Getting Started in

SWING TRADING

The *Getting Started In* Series

Getting Started in Online Day Trading by Kassandra Bentley
Getting Started in Asset Allocation by Bill Bresnan and Eric P. Gelb
Getting Started in Online Investing by David L. Brown
    and Kassandra Bentley
Getting Started in Investment Clubs by Marsha Bertrand
Getting Started in Stocks by Alvin D. Hall
Getting Started in Mutual Funds by Alvin D. Hall
Getting Started in Estate Planning by Kerry Hannon
Getting Started in 401(k) Investing by Paul Katzeff
Getting Started in Internet Investing by Paul Katzeff
Getting Started in Security Analysis by Peter J. Klein
Getting Started in Global Investing by Robert P. Kreitler
Getting Started in Futures by Todd Lofton
Getting Started in Financial Information by Daniel Moreau
    and Tracey Longo
Getting Started in Technical Analysis by Jack D. Schwager
Getting Started in Hedge Funds by Daniel A. Strachman
Getting Started in Rental Income by Michael C. Thomsett
Getting Started in Property Flipping by Michael C. Thomsett
Getting Started in Fundamental Analysis by Michael C. Thomsett
Getting Started in Six Sigma by Michael C. Thomsett
Getting Started in Options by Michael C. Thomsett
Getting Started in Real Estate Investing by Michael C. Thomsett
    and Jean Freestone Thomsett
Getting Started in Annuities by Gordon M. Williamson
Getting Started in Bonds by Sharon Saltzgiver Wright

Getting Started in

SWING TRADING

Michael C. Thomsett

John Wiley & Sons, Inc.

Published by John Wiley & Sons, Inc., Hoboken, New Jersey.

Published simultaneously in Canada.

For general information on our other products and services or for technical support, please contact our Customer Care Department within the United States at (800) 762-2974, outside the United States at (317) 572-3993 or fax (317) 572-4002.

Wiley also publishes its books in a variety of electronic formats. Some content that appears in print may not be available in electronic books. For more information about Wiley products, visit our website at www.wiley.com.

Library of Congress Cataloging-in-Publication Data:

Thomsett, Michael C.
  Getting started in swing trading / Michael C. Thomsett.
      p. cm.
  Includes index.
  ISBN-13: 978-0-470-08461-8 (pbk.)
  ISBN-10: 0-470-08461-8 (pbk.)
  1. Investment analysis. 2. Stocks. 3. Speculation—Psychological aspects. I. Title.
  HG4529.T488 2007
  332.63'2042—dc22

                              2006033462

Printed in the United States of America.

10 9 8 7 6 5 4 3 2 1

CONTENTS

Introduction: Why Swing Trading Makes Sense Today   vii

Chapter 1
The Big Picture: How Swing Trading Works   1

Chapter 2
The Basic Technical Rules   23

Chapter 3
Candlestick Charting for Swing Trading   45

Chapter 4
Reaction Swings and the Reaction Cycle   65

Chapter 5
Brokerage Rules and the Pattern Day Trader   87

Chapter 6
Picking Stocks for Swing Trading   103

Chapter 7
Selling Short: Entering a Swing Trade with a Short Order   125

Chapter 8
Options for Swing Trading: the Basics   135

Chapter 9

Option Strategies for Swing Trading   **159**

Chapter 10

Swing Trading in Your Investment Portfolio   **179**

Glossary   **197**

Index   **209**

Why Swing Trading Makes Sense Today

S wing trading is not a new idea. It has only recently become a viable strategy for the average investor. Before the Internet opened up markets to virtually everyone, only the select few with access to an exchange trading floor could make short-term trades in and out of positions on a daily basis.

In that pre-Internet era, real-time quotes or online charting services simply did not exist. To get a quote on a stock, you would have to telephone a stockbroker, leave a message, and hope your call was returned before the market closed. It was impossible to track stock prices throughout the day because, again, you needed the stockbroker who had exclusive access to price information. So *swing trading*—movement in and out of positions to take advantage of short-term price movements—was just not possible.

In the 1980s stockbrokers began relying on a primitive version of automated access to exchange floors. An old system, *Quotron*, provided brokers with desktop PCs to get quotes in much faster time than ever before. This was revolutionary. Those brokers with Quotron machines had a distinct advantage over those brokers who depended on delayed quotes and telephone or ticker-based quotes on exchange floors.

Even the revolution of providing stockbrokers with their own direct access, pales in comparison to today's environment. Stockbrokers are, essentially, obsolete. Any trader who knows enough about investing and who knows how to execute a trade is likely to use an online discount brokerage service, which is so incredibly easy that traditional brokerage services are of questionable value. The traditional firms have emphasized the need for professional advice from their "analysts," but the track record is dismal. Not only have analysts' recommendations underperformed the market; in some cases, investors would have done better to do the exact opposite of the suggestions offered to them.

Today, the old-style stockbroker has quietly faded away to be replaced with the combination of analysts and subscription services. The claim that these services provide some kind of valuable information is dubious. In fact, investors now get superior *free* information from online brokerage services and do not need to pay for help. For example, the most successful discount brokerage firm, Charles Schwab, provides its traders with free access to Standard & Poor's Stock Reports, Reuters Research Ratings, and Schwab's own Equity Rating service all for thousands of publicly listed companies.

Informed investors—those most likely to be attracted to short-term strategies such as swing trading—are the least likely to depend on advice from others. Historically, advice from stockbrokers, financial advisors and analysts has been very poor, and today's individual investor is more likely than ever before to want to proceed without help or advice from a commission-based or subscription-based person or company.

This book is addressed to the investor who recognizes the limitations of depending on others for investment advice; who is willing to learn the essential steps needed to invest on his or her own; and who wants to master proven strategies.

No one can show you how to get rich quick and with no risk. Those kinds of promises are vacant and unfounded. But it is possible to increase your rate of successes by utilizing strategies that give you an edge and help to anticipate the next price direction. There is no "sure-fire" method to achieving 100 percent profits. But swing trading can improve your rate of success, your timing, and your overall profitability.

This book also answers the question of what products to use in swing trading. Most people simply assume that you must use stocks to take long or short positions in stocks as part of a swing trading strategy. This topic is covered in depth. Realistically, however, buying and selling shares of stocks is a limited strategy because you are restricted to investing by a limited pool of capital. Later in this book, you will discover ways to expand your swing trading potential with less money and lower risk. You will also see how to take up positions when you expect stock to trend downward but without having to sell stock short. This high-risk strategy is not the only way, or even the best or most affordable way, to play a bear market.

So while you learn about swing trading, you will also expand your understanding of market risk, gaining insight into alternative ways to invest, and improving your knowledge base in the market. Swing trading is a short-term technical strategy. That does not mean it has to be high-risk or appropriate only for the most experienced or wealthiest investors. It is a strategy that can be useful to anyone as long as the basic realities of risk, timing, and methods of investing are mastered and observed.

The Big Picture
How Swing Trading Works

Everyone knows that big institutional investors such as mutual funds have a tremendous advantage over the individual investor—more money, better research, broad diversification. In some respects, however, you have an advantage over the big institutions. They cannot make decisions quickly in the market; pay attention to the subtle, short-term price gyrations that characterize market cycles; or watch only a few key stocks. The big institutions have to take a shotgun approach to investing, just because of their size.

You probably don't have millions of dollars in your portfolio and you don't have to answer to anyone else. This flexibility and mobility is your advantage; and this is where you can benefit from *swing trading* strategies. With swing trading, you operate within a very limited window, two to five days worth of activity in most cases.

You will observe that stock price movement in the short term tends to react (or more specifically, to overreact) to each and every market event. This range of events includes trading volume, broader market activity, and all financial, economic and political news. Later in this chapter, this tendency of

swing trading
a strategy that involves two- to five-day market cycles and identifies high and low points in short-term cycles; and flags key points for moving in and out of stock positions based on specific chart pattern signals.

efficient market hypothesis

the theory that pricing of stocks reflects all information currently known by investors at any given time, resulting in the conclusion that all stock prices are fair and reasonable.

random walk theory

a belief that all pricing of stocks is random, and that at any time there is a 50/50 chance that a stock's price will either rise or fall. This theory discounts the value of fundamental analysis and assumes that stock pricing is a battle between buyers and sellers for purely technical reasons.

stock prices is explained in the context of the three dominant emotions that literally rule the market: greed, fear and uncertainty.

Short-term price movement can be defined and anticipated in terms of these three emotions, and this is where you gain your swing trading advantage. Rather than making decisions based of greed, fear and uncertainty, swing trading is a technique based on logic and analysis rather than on emotion. An old adage about the market states that "bull and bears can make profits, but pigs and chickens cannot." This is entirely true. You can make profits in all types of markets, but only if you are able to see past the emotional reactions that govern the thinking of the majority.

In fact, those emotions largely determine and cause those short-term price changes in the market. The fact that short-term pricing is chaotic disproves the *efficient market hypothesis*, the belief that all pricing of stocks reflects everything that is publicly known at any given time. The reality proves that this is untrue.

The efficient market might exist on a different level. For example, the long-term averages of price movement may occur on some level of efficiency, but the two- to five-day movement of price is virtually caused completely by those three troubling emotions and their domination of market thinking.

So it is reasonable to believe that the efficient market hypothesis might be a valid theory over the long-term, but not in the short-term. The opposite is true of another market concept, the *random walk theory*. This is a more fatalistic view of the market. The random walk is a belief that at any given time, there is a 50/50 chance that a stock's price will rise or fall. The whole pricing of stocks is believed to be completely random.

The random walk accurately describes the two- to five-day tendency of stocks. Short-term pricing is obviously responsive to emotional overreaction and illogic. However, over the long term, an analysis of stock pricing

Key Point
Swing traders observe how emotions affect price, and act when those emotions exaggerate a trend to present a profit opportunity.

demonstrates a clear connection between strong fundamentals and strong price growth (or, on the other hand, weak fundamentals leading to price deterioration). So the two major theories can be quite instructive in understanding both short-term and long-term stock pricing:

1. The efficient market hypothesis makes sense but only over the long term. For the short-term pricing of stocks, there is no apparent efficiency involved; stock pricing changes due to emotional effects.

2. The random walk theory makes perfect sense in the two- to five-day window and perfectly describes the way that stocks behave. However, it is not so much a random event, but the outcome of a struggle between the greed and fear of investors (with uncertainty representing a stalemate between the two). However, over the long term, the random walk theory falls apart.

An Overview: The Basic Definitions

Any approach you take in the market will determine your success, of course. But there is a tendency among investors to believe that some systems are effective in ensuring consistent profits, and this is simply not true. Timing is the key to profits. While picking fundamentally strong stocks is essential, of course, it is timing more than anything else that determines whether your decisions create profits or losses.

Most people who buy shares of stock automatically assume that the price they pay is a "starting point" or the "zero base" of their investment. From that zero base price the stock is supposed to rise. But as everyone who has put money into stocks already knows, the stock's price sometimes falls.

Key Point

Everyone tends to believe that their purchase price is the starting point in a stock's price. Realistically, though, it might be midway through a trend or at the trend's very peak.

---

fundamental analysis
the valuation of stocks based on a company's financial strength, earnings, and trends, including assessment of working capital, equity and debt capitalization, and operating results.

technical analysis
the study of stock price and volume trends, charts, and trading patterns, for the purpose of anticipating short-term price movement to time trades.

The system you employ to pick stocks may serve as your real starting point; the strategy you employ controls the timing for putting your strategy into place. This is the primary difference. It does not matter whether you are a believer in *fundamental analysis* or *technical analysis*. The rule remains the same: the method is used to isolate those stocks you want to trade, and the strategy controls the timing of your decision. Swing trading provides you with one effective strategy.

Swing traders use the timing of short-term trading patterns to take advantage of the tendencies of stock prices. These tendencies are to trade in brief waves (thus, the importance of the two- to five-day time span) in which stock prices rise and fall. After specific patterns and signals occur, a reversal often takes place and this is where swing trading becomes a powerful timing strategy.

The swing trader recognizes these patterns. After a stock's price has risen in a specific pattern (in the movement of the price, the price distance in a day's trading range, and the volume), the swing trader recognizes a sell signal. After the price falls in a specific pattern, the swing trader moves in and buys. This timing goes in opposition to the most recent price pattern, and is aimed at anticipating a reversal. The natural tendency for pricing is to operate in these short-term back-and-forth cycles. Because swing trading involves timing a trade in anticipation that prices are going to go the opposite, way, swing trading is a short-term form of *contrarian investing*.

Key Point

When investors respond to greed and fear, they tend to buy high and sell how. Swing traders are able to respond unemotionally, and achieve the opposite: Buy low and sell high.

Typically, traders tend to be reactive rather than contrarian. So when people see a stock moving up, they want to buy; and when they see it moving down, they want to sell. Swing traders, in comparison, are faithful to the best-known market advice: *Buy low and sell high.* The unfortunate truth is that the majority of investors do exactly the opposite. They buy when prices have moved higher out of greed, and they sell when prices fall, out of fear. Swing trading is a strategy for short-term trading that puts the concept of "buy low and sell high" into effect.

Contrarian investing in practice is far more complex than the timing of trades. The contrarian interprets both fundamental and technical signals in ways dissimilar to the common thinking seen in the market. Timing is only one aspect to the contrarian point of view; but for swing traders it is a critical point.

contrarian investing

an approach to investing based on the assumption that the majority is more often wrong than right in its buy and sell decisions, and that timing will be improved by taking actions opposite the market as a whole.

The struggle between "crowd mentality" of the market and the contrarian view extends as well to philosophies about which kind of data to employ for decisions. The fundamental view (adherence to recent historical financial results as the basis for making trades) and the technical view (based on price movement and patterns to anticipate the next move or series of moves) are not always at odds. Although swing trading is a purely technical strategy, it can be employed in a manner that combines both fundamental and technical indicators. The distinction should be kept clear: picking specific stocks is not the same as timing buy and sell decisions. With that in mind, you may consider using the fundamentals to pick a range of stocks you want to trade; and then use swing trading and other technical tools to actually time your decisions.

Too often, investors are asked to choose between fundamental and technical schools of thought. It makes more sense to use both. Both approaches may limit your view of what is occurring in the market; and both sides contain flows. Fundamentals are strictly historical and may be outdated by the time you need to make a decision. Technical indicators are invariably short-term in nature and short-term indicators are historically unreliable for long-term investing.

The lesson to learn from this is that both fundamental and technical sides are going to contain flaws, but both contain useful aspects. Either theory should be dependent on a study of trends, both short-term and long-term. The trend is the key to picking stocks and to timing buy and sell decisions.

Swing Trading, Day Trading, and Long-Term Hold Strategies

speculators

individuals willing to take greater than average risks in exchange for the opportunity for higher than average profits.

long-term hold

description of a strategy for portfolio management, involving selection of stocks with the intention of holding shares for many years in order to build a secure base for long-term growth.

There are many ways to invest in the market. The most conservative investors want low volatility and slow but steady growth; *speculators* welcome volatile stocks and the unsure future because such stocks exhibit broader price swings. A speculator welcomes higher risk in recognition of the inescapable relationship between risk and profit. With few exceptions, risk and profit are two sides of the same market coin.

The most conservative position within the market is selection of a company perceived to be safe. This normally means that capitalization is high; the company has been in business for many decades; and the company dominates its sector. Such companies have grown over the long term but only slowly and steadily. The conservative *long-term hold* is far from exciting, but it does create a solid, safe base for your portfolio.

On the opposite side of the risk spectrum is the highly speculative approach. People in this part of the market buy penny stocks, IPOs, and highly-volatile issues; trade options to achieve leverage; and may even

---

Key Point

Conservative investing is safer than high-risk; but it also offers far lower opportunities for profit. The elements of *risk* and *profit* are directly related and cannot be separated.

---

combine high-risk stock trades with index investments, commodities trading, and stock futures. These are very exotic forms of risk, and only those who thoroughly understand the market *and* the risks themselves should be involved. To a degree, swing traders may want to employ options as part of their strategy (this is explored in later chapters). But options can be employed in relatively safe ways to leverage money without exposing yourself to the possibility of huge losses. That is the distinction between a swing trader's use of instruments like options, versus pure speculation. A speculator intentionally exposes capital to the risk of loss, but a swing trader uses options to limit losses and to leverage capital.

Somewhere in between these extremes is the *day trader*. This is a trader who intentionally moves capital in and out of stock positions in the extreme short-term, usually within a single trading day. Day traders are also usually high-volume traders, executing numerous daily trades in more than one stock; or many trades in the same stock. If an individual buys and sells the same stock on very high volume (four times or more within five consecutive days), they are classified as a *pattern day trader* by the Securities and Exchange Commission (SEC) and are subject to special rules for cash held in a trading account.

The swing trader is likely to belong closer to the side of the speculator than that of the conservative investor. This does not mean that swing trading is necessarily high-risk in comparison to other strategies. You can limit your capital exposure to

day trader
an individual who executes trades within a single day or over the shortest possible time, often moving in and out of positions within a matter of hours and employing a high volume of trading activity.

pattern day trader
as defined by the SEC, any trader who buys or sells a single stock four or more times within five days; a pattern day trader must maintain no less than $25,000 account equity before a high volume of trading is permitted.

swing trading, your volume of trades, and the number of stocks you swing trade—all to reduce overall risk or to limit your exposure. But in the spectrum of investing, everyone should be able to identify where a specific strategy belongs.

Any strategy may also be used in combination with other strategies with dissimilar risk characteristics. Diversifying by risk is a wise and effective way to manage your portfolio. For example, you may have the majority of your capital invested in your own home, certificates of deposit, and Blue Chip stocks; and use a relatively small portion of your capital for swing trading and other strategies.

The Swing Trade Approach: The Strategy in a Nutshell

The precise method of swing trading is going to vary among individuals. Everyone has their favorite variation on any strategy. If you have observed how people behave in the market, you also know that investors are at times ingenious, at other times irrational, emotional, or unrealistically hopeful. The "what if" factor is always present.

Swing trading is a process of fixing a series of "rules" that trigger a trade decision. It is based on the study of stock price patterns over a short period of time, the two- to five-day window. Because swing traders recognize that short-term price swings reflect investor emotions, they trade in a unique manner. Rather than trading the stock, swing traders time their decisions to trade the emotions that dominate the market. This does not mean that the stock's fundamentals are unimportant. In fact, a starting point should be to narrow a list of stocks you will swing trade, based on both fundamental and technical analysis. These may be at conflict to a degree. The purpose of using the fundamentals is not to find the safest stocks because these will not be good candidates for swing trading.

Key Point

The market is characterized by prevailing myths. The beliefs of many investors and traders are provably irrational in many cases, but continue to be widely believed. For example, there really is no "system" for creating 100% profits.

Key Point
It makes sense to be flexible. You might start out swing trading only to realize that a stock is a solid long-term hold. In that case, buying the stock makes sense ... and does not prevent you from continuing to swing trade in the stock as well.

The "ideal" stock is one with strong fundamentals (excellent management, long-term growth history, etc.) but with short-term volatile technical signals. This means, of course, that the trading range (the distance between typical high and low prices) is broader than the average stocks.

So swing traders need well managed companies whose stocks are somewhat volatile. This is a middle ground; many well managed companies experience short-term volatility because they are in the news; earnings are uncertain; or product news may cause the stock to rise or fall, or to do both in turn. So if you must define the ideal stock for swing trading, it would be one with strong long-term fundamentals and very volatile short-term technical signals.

The majority of investors are not well informed; and this is where you have the advantage as a swing trader. In the environment where greed and fear dominate decision-making, you are matched up against people who will be willing to buy stock from you at too high a price; or who will sell stock to you at a bargain price. You recognize these tendencies by tracking the daily chart patterns and identifying the turning points and reacting to the reversal signals you find through swing trading. As a swing trader, you benefit from the way that most people make decisions—impulsively, emotionally, and at the wrong time.

Most people buy when they should sell and sell when they should buy. Swing trading may be thought of a technique for trading emotions (or even trading people and their tendency to react with the emotions of greed and fear). In some respects, this means that it doesn't really matter which stocks you trade, because the technique applies to all stocks and to all short-term price trends. But because stocks are different, it remains a wise idea to identify a range of stocks by attribute that are best suited for (a) short-term swing trading based on an appropriate volatility level and (b) long-term safety based on strong fundamentals. This is sound advice because some swing traders decide to hold onto their stocks even when the original plan was to swing trade. If you are going to end up keeping some of the stock you buy, it should be high-quality stock from a long-term perspective.

Using the swing trading technique, you identify some very specific short-term trends. While day traders watch price movement moment to moment, swing traders normally base their timing decisions on end-of-day chart patterns. The two-to five-day window is based on the theory that a day's trends are revealing. This means that the opening and closing price, the trading range and the breadth of that range (distance from top to bottom price) are all important in executing a swing trade. For example, one day might have an opening and closing price close to the day's highest and lowest price levels; and another day might have very little gap between opening and closing price, but demonstrate a lot of action in between, with prices moving far above and below the actual open and close price levels.

uptrend

a movement in a stock's price to the upside; for swing traders, an uptrend is defined as three or more consecutive days in which the closing price was higher than the opening price.

downtrend

a movement in a stock's price to the downside; for swing traders, a downtrend is defined as three or more consecutive days in which the closing price was lower than the opening price.

A "swing" is a change in direction. So a stock that has been trending upward will swing to the downward, and vice versa. A swing trader uses the charting techniques involving open, close, and trading range to recognize when such swings are most likely to occur. Daily volume is also significant in the mix of signals that you will come to depend on in developing your swing trading strategy.

Within this short-term daily trend watching, the direction of each day's price movement is also important. By definition, a swing is most likely to occur when the open and close of the stock has been occurring in the same direction. This means that in an existing *uptrend*, the day's close should be higher than the open for at least three consecutive days before the trend can be relied upon to put a trade into action. And when the price trend is downward, by definition, a *downtrend* requires that for at least three days in a row, the closing price was lower than the opening price. So the overall *price range* of a day's history is not enough; the direction of price movement must confirm the apparent trend as well.

> ## Key Point
>
> There is a distinct difference between traditional market primary and secondary trends on the one hand, and very short-tern price trends on the other. Swing traders limit their analysis to a two- to five-day window.

The uptrend and downtrend used by swing traders are not the same as the more universally recognized market trends. Technicians track trends in stocks as well as various indices and these are well known. They also use moving averages of various configurations to signal or anticipate major uptrends and downtrends. The short-term trends described above and used in swing trading are entirely different.

price range
the overall range of a stock's price within a single day, from highest price attained down to lowest price, and distinct from opening and closing prices.

This explains as well why swing traders usually stick to the complete trend of a single trading day. When you first consider this guideline, it does not appear to make sense. A valid question may be, "Shouldn't the decision be made when trading patterns are met rather than at the end of a trading day?" The answer, of course, is that any strategy should be as flexible as you need it to be. There is no hard-and-fast *requirement* that trading occur only when a day's trading has been completed. However, swing traders have discovered that while their timing of trades may be flexible, the complete day is most revealing. Patterns emerge during a trading day based on the time of day and overall direction of the market. Many technicians, for example, give great importance to trends established in the first hour, or the first two hours. A specific stock's final hours of trading may be largely influenced by overall market trends on the day.

In order to establish the trend for purposes of swing trading, the full day is considered the template and also makes comparisons uniform. This is always useful in any type of price analysis. In addition, another important type of signal may be found between the close of one day and the open of the next day. Swing traders, like many other technicians, are likely to assign importance when price changes between the two days show large gaps, or when a low-volume day is followed by a high-volume day. These are examples of the kind of changes occurring between days that will be viewed as important to swing traders, and it further supports the belief that to establish the two- to five-day window to identify a swing trading opportunity, you need to have the complete day and not just hour-to-hour change. A day trader is inclined toward recognizing and grabbing profitable opportunities as they occur, but day trading is a far less sophisticated market strategy than swing trading. So while some traders may prefer the excitement of continually watching a stock's price during the day, swing traders employ a more methodical system.

Chapters 3 and 4 provide you with a far more detailed explanation of the exact signals and methods of finding them. The purpose here is to provide you with an overview of how swing trading works and how you can use short-term trends to zero in on profit opportunities.

The basic swing trading rule is to act after three or more consistent signals occur. When the price has been moving to the upside, the signal is to sell; and when price has been moving to the downside, the signal is to buy. Remember, the *swing* is the key. The theory of swing trading is based on the belief that short-term price change occurs in predictable rhythms and cycles. Upward movement is followed by downward movement in these short-term trends, and vice versa.

There are several attributes required in order for these "rules" of swing trading to go into effect. These are:

1. *Recognize an uptrend.* A true two-to five-day trend consists of a specific pattern in opening and closing prices. In an uptrend, each day should exhibit a series of higher highs, offset by a series of higher lows. So each day's price passes the previous day's peak on the upside; and each drop is less than the previous day. Figure 1.1 illustrates this principle on a simplified line graph; note that the trend lines for both high and low price levels conforms to the uptrend rule.

2. *Recognize a downtrend.* The downtrend also develops over a two- to five-day period. But it is characterized by a series of lower highs and lower lows. So each day's high will be lower than the previous day; and each day's low is lower than the previous day. The swing trading downtrend is shown in Figure 1.2. This figure shows the swing trading downtrend; the high prices are progressively lower each day, and the offsetting low prices are lower as well.

Key Point

Swing trading is so called because of the tendency for price to swing back and forth in a two- to five-day window. This occurs because day-to-day trading is dominated by emotion.

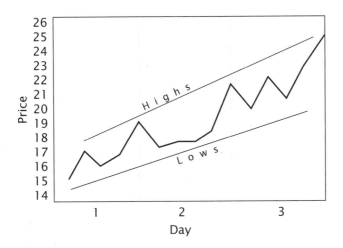

FIGURE 1.1   The Uptrend

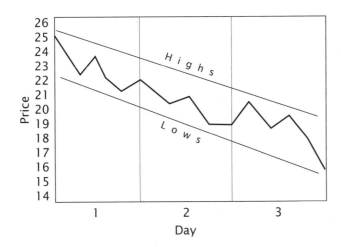

FIGURE 1.2   The Downtrend

setup

a signal to act in a swing trade pattern; the setup at the top of an uptrend is a sell signal, the setup at the bottom of a downtrend is a buy signal.

narrow range day

a day in which the high-to-low price of a day is much smaller than the typical day, and when it occurs after three or more established trend day patterns.

3. *Identify a setup.* The *setup* is a signal that it is time to take action. The setup at the top of the two-to five-day uptrend is a sell signal. And the setup at the end of a two- to five-day downtrend is a buy signal. In other words, the swing trade is premised on the idea that these specific signals can be used to time decisions and to profit from the cyclical swings in price.

4. *Look for the narrow range day.* All signals are stronger when they are confirmed. The *narrow range day* is a day in which the distance from high to low price is much smaller than preceding "typical trading ranges. For example, if a stock has been trading in a range of two to three points and the two- to five-day trend is established, a narrow range day at the end of the established trend is a strong confirming signal.

Remember that the narrow range day pattern is important only after a substantial price move. A typical narrow range day at the end of a downtrend is a strong buy signal. This is illustrated in Figure 1.3.

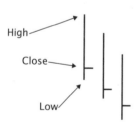

Typical
Trading Days

Narrow
Range Day

FIGURE 1.3 Typical Trading Days and Narrow Range Day

5. *Keep an eye on changes in volume.* Stocks tend to trade with "typical" daily volume, but when that level changes it often signals a change in the interaction between buyers and sellers. For swing trading, an exceptionally high-volume day *accompanied by a narrow range day* is a strong signal to act. So when the breadth of trading narrows and volume increases substantially, that signals that the established trend is probably on the verge of reversing.

These signals should be used in conjunction with one another. When a two-to five-day uptrend has been established, look for the setup. *Confirmation* is a very important concept in swing trading: when you are able to confirm the trend with a setup, you have an exceptionally strong buy or sell signal. The confirming indicators are a narrow range day and increased trading volume. When you see both of these together, you have exceptionally strong confirmation that it is time to act (to sell after the uptrend or to buy after the downtrend).

confirmation
a signal that provides additional indication to another signal, that reinforces the indicated timing of a buy or sell move.

The Theory of Chart-Watching

There are two general schools of thought about how to pick stocks and time buy and sell decisions. The fundamental school relies on financial reports and trends and the technical school of thought bases these decisions on price.

Key Point

There is no reason to shun one type of analysis and favor the other. You can gain valuable insight from both fundamental and technical analysis.

OHLC chart

a type of stock chart summarizing the open, high, low, and close for a day using a single vertical line and two horizontal tabs. The top of the vertical line is the line and the bottom is the low; the left tab is the day's opening price and the right tab is the day's closing price.

point-and-figure chart

a stock chart reflecting rising prices with columns of Xs extending from high to low price; and columns of stack's Xs. This chart does not distinguish trading days, only trends.

While both points of view have merit, it makes sense to use not one or the other, but both in tandem. Swing trading is a technical strategy, but the stocks you pick to use for swing trading may be selected based on fundamental strength. To the extent that you are going to rely on technical signals, you will use charts as a primary timing tool. Investors use many different kinds of charts, the most popular being the *OHLC chart*. This consists of a vertical line extending from the high to low price for a day; and two horizontal tabs. The one appearing to the left is the day's opening price, and the one to the right is the day's closing price. This type of charting tool is illustrated in Figure 1-4.

The OHLC chart is popular because using only three lines, it conveys the essential information about activity over a period of time. This is efficient. A more obscure chart is the *point- and-figure chart*. This consists of stacks of Xs and Os without any regard for the time involved. The Xs are shown when the price rose, and the Os when the price fell. This chart gives technicians a quick view of trading range trends, but for most investors it is not as easy to use as the OHLC chart.

Time is usually important to traders in order to make sound judgments for their stock decisions; for this reason, the point and figure chart provides a particular kind of information for some purposes, but is not as valuable as the OHLC. Today's charting services invariably include a *moving average* as

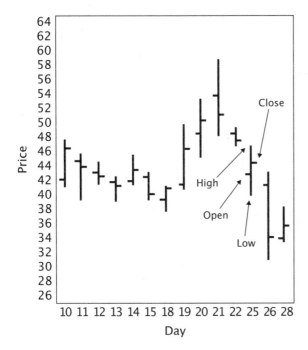

FIGURE 1.4 The OHLC Chart

well as daily changes in the stock's price. In addition to showing the important open, high, low and close price points, charts also include one or more moving average lines. The most popular are 200-day and 50-day moving averages. These do away with the distractions of short-term volatility and show how a stock's price has evolved over time.

A final type of chart, and one used in coming chapters in this book, is the candlestick chart. This descriptive term is given because each day's trading has a body that is either white or black, with vertical lines extending above and below the main body. This type of chart was developed in 18th Century Japan to track rice prices. In the 20th Century, U.S. technical analysts and chartists began to recognize the value of candlesticks for tracking the OHLC but also to get an immediate picture of whether a trend is moving upward or downward. Chapter three explains candlesticks in detail.

moving average
a statistical method of showing a trend that is representative of changes without short-term volatility. The average is computed by adding up the fields in the period, and then dividing by the number of trading days.

Key Point

Charts display the short-term tendency of prices to swing back and forth. These trends are not erratic or random; they reflect visually the dominate market forces of greed, fear and uncertainty.

Charts all summarize the flow and pattern to a stock's price cycles, both short-term and long-term. There is a natural rhythm to price trends that reflects the interaction between buyers and sellers *and* the dominance of one of the three market emotions: greed, fear and uncertainty.

Technicians may consider themselves to be *chartists*, people who rely on specific price patterns to predict the next direction of a stock's price. Chapter two explores the many popular charting signals and explains how to recognize them. The chartist tends to believe that fundamental analysis has limited value because it is historical and does not affect the forces of supply and demand that determine price movement. Some chartists acknowledge that long-term trends are dominated by fundamental strength or weakness of a company, but rely on chart price patterns for the short term.

chartists
technical analysts who rely primarily on recognition of specific price patterns and short-term trends to predict and anticipate the next price direction in a stock's price.

There are both pro and con arguments concerning taking the chartist's approach. On the positive side, the pattern of price movement does contain a specific predictability. This is not the same as a guarantee, but there is a tendency for price to move in a pattern. Swing trading is a typical charting strategy because it is designed to observe and predict price movement. When prices move in one direction and in specific ways for three or more trading days, the tendency is for price to then reverse and go in the opposite direction. Because you cannot know how many periods a trend involves, swing traders look for reversal signals in order to time their decisions.

> **Key Point**
>
> No investment decisions should be made in isolation. Fundamental information is not merely historical; it also indicates whether a company is financially sound—or even solvent—today.

Chartists believe that buyers and sellers continually interact. When a stock's price rises far enough, current owners want to sell to take profits; and that causes the price to fall. When price falls far enough, the stock becomes a bargain so new buyers place orders. The outcome of this never-ending interaction is the two- to five-day wave action of stocks.

On the negative side, charting is focused only on price and volume and those who track price movement may ignore fundamental news. This is a mistake. For example, in spite of how a stock's price patterns evolve, when a company misses a deadline for filing a financial report that is a danger signal. For example, in October 2005 Krispy Kreme (the doughnut chain) stock fell below $6 per share and the stock chart may have looked to some chartists like a buying opportunity. But something more profound was going on. The company had missed its filing deadline with the SEC and it was disclosed that improper accounting practices had been in place for several years. The company's stock recovered somewhat by late 2006 but continued to report quarterly losses. In this situation—where profound fundamental problems were evident—relying strictly on chart patterns would have been a mistake.

Chartists do better when they combine fundamental and technical signals. You may use charts as a primary timing mechanism for short-term swing trading; but selection of stocks for this play should be made based on at least a preliminary review of fundamental issues:

- Is the company solvent?
- Has a profit been reported (recently or, more significantly, ever)?
- How much debt is the company carrying?
- Does the company compete well within its industry sector?

Even without looking at a financial statement, you can learn a lot just by reading the recent headlines. Online brokerage services provide news for each company. For example, if you research Krispy Kreme (KKD) on Charles Schwab & Company's brokerage service—*https://investing.schwab.com*—you find the stock price, reports of rating services, comparative price performance data, and recent news headlines. Obviously, using both fundamental and technical information provides fast and reliable information, and vastly improves a chartist's information base.

The Primary Emotions: Fear, Greed and Uncertainty

Chartists employing a variety of strategies will usually agree on one premise: Short-term price movement is predictable most of the time. Some chartists depend entirely on some specific patterns and tests within a price pattern. Others, like swing traders, believe that the cornerstone of the strategy is the three-part emotional trend that rules how most of the market works. So greed, fear and uncertainty determine price patterns and make it easier to time and predict price movement.

Some swing traders describe the strategy as one that trades emotions, not stocks. But this is not entirely true. A wise trader will always be aware that stock selection is key to a smart program, so a starting point should be to pick stocks that are going to act and react to the normal market forces. If you pick a distressed stock (such as that Krispy Kreme in 2005) or a stock that has risen in value beyond any fundamental explanation (like Amazon.com or eBay in the recent past), you cannot rely on the normal cyclical patterns of short-term charting; so those situations may not provide reliable signals either. Later in this book, you will find guidelines for picking stocks for swing trading.

Once you have limited your range of potential swing trading stocks, the timing of trades can be based on the three emotions that rule the market. Market observers and the financial news media like to give names to these emotional trends other than the raw emotional names. When greed is in control, it is called a *rally*. When fear dominates and prices begin to fall, it is called a *correction*. And when a period of uncertainty is dominant, that is referred to as a period of *consolidation*. The three market conditions are summarized in Figure 1.5.

rally
a period when prices are rising, also known as a condition where greed dominates the market.

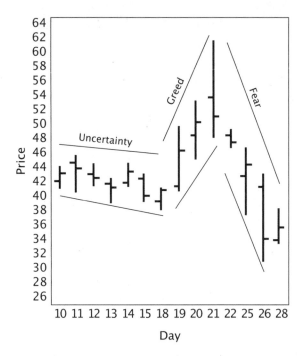

FIGURE 1.5   Emotions and the Market

The consolidation period—when uncertainty rules—is sometimes described by analysts as a time of "agreement." In other words, under this interpretation, the current price range is agreeable to both sellers and buyers. This is inaccurate. It is not a time of agreement at all, but rather a time when neither buyers nor sellers dominate the market. During periods of uncertainty, the buying and selling activity tends to be well matched, so that no changes in supply or demand are evident. There is no agreement at all; both sides have no idea where the stock's price is going to go next.

In all three market conditions—characterized by the emotions of greed, fear and uncertainty—one fact remains constant: most traders do not learn from their past mistakes. Logically, everyone knows that no direction remains forever. When a stock's price begins to rise, there is going to be a limit but greed ignores this. When the price is

correction
the description of a market in which prices are falling, when the emotion of fear dominates the market.

consolidation
a time when price is not moving upward or downward, but remaining within a narrow trading range; a market dominated by uncertainty.

Key Point

The market likes to give exciting names to upward-trending prices, and to soften downward-trending prices. Thus you hear about a rally (up market) versus profit-taking (down market); or enthusiasm (up market) versus caution (down market).

---

falling, it cannot fall forever and at some point shares drop to a bargain price level, but fear ignores that fact. And when uncertainty rules the market (even if for only a few days) traders tend to become impatient. They either lose interest in the stock or make an uninformed decision which is likely to be wrong at least 50 percent of the time. So holders will sell right before prices rise at the end of the uncertainty, or they buy right before prices fall. These actions occur because traders act impulsively and emotionally. So with this in mind, you may add a fourth emotion: impatience. The impatient investor acts too quickly and makes a lot of timing mistakes.

Swing traders manage their emotions and simply observe the interaction between the emotions of other traders and market prices. This contrarian approach is more sophisticated than the common definition. A swing trading contrarian does not simply buy when most people are selling and vice verse; the more advanced version involves making decisions contrary to the dominant emotion of the moment. When prices peak in a frenzy of greed, the swing trader looks for the sell signal. When prices fall rapidly in the ravages of fear, the swing trader remains calm and looks for the signal that the price has bottomed out. When uncertainty is the dominant emotion, swing traders resist the temptation to "do something" and remain patient until a signal emerges.

Before delving into more about specific swing trading examples, you need to review the basic rules of technical analysis and chart interpretation. The next chapter goes through these basics as a building block to turning swing trading into a powerful market tool.

Chapter 2

The Basic Technical Rules

The tools used in technical analysis are price-related for the most part. They are visual in nature. Trading and price patterns are given great weight by technicians. In comparison, fundamental analysis is a numerical study using financial results to establish recent trends and to predict future value—and thus price growth.

While fundamental analysis is backward-looking, technical analysis is intended to anticipate future price trends. Investors may use both of these approaches effectively to improve identification of risk, stock selection, and the timing of decisions:

1. *Identification of risk.* When people hear about risk, they tend to think of only one kind of risk—losing money versus making money. This is *market risk* and every stock investor faces this risk continually. The identification of this risk is elusive, however, because so many aspects of the company and the stock have to be considered. Chapter 6 explores the question of how to pick stocks based on financial condition

market risk
the risk that a stock's value will fall rather than rise (or rise after an investor sells). Market risk can be compared and judged based on fundamental trends and technical price history.

volatility

the degree of movement in a stock's price, and the number of points of movement from day to day. The greater the price swing, the higher a stock's volatility. Most investors define market risk in terms of price volatility.

trading range

the normal trading area extending from the highest to the lowest typical price. Stocks tend to trade within a specific range. The broader the range, the greater the volatility and thus the greater the market risk.

and capitalization; and those questions are the starting point for identifying market risk.

Technical analysis includes comparisons of price and *volatility*, which is another aspect to market risk. The ideal swing trade stock is one with a degree of volatility. The price swings are required to achieve the variation needed in swing trading, so a very low-volatility stock will not work. On the other end of the spectrum, highly volatile stocks are unpredictable and not suitable for most swing trading. The most suitable stocks, based on market risk, are those that tend to be moderately volatile, and that trade within more than just a few points' *trading range*.

2. *Stock selection.* Picking stocks is, of course, the determining step in whether you achieve profits or suffer losses. There is a tendency among investors to use methods for stock selection based on rudimentary technical signs, but these are often wrong. For example, some people buy stock because the price has been climbing recently, or they sell shares that they already own because the price has fallen. A rational method for stock selection may include fundamental analysis and a thorough study of some key financial ratios and trends; and technical analysis for the timing of trades, among which swing trading is one of the most effective.

Key Point

Swing trading requires a moderate degree of volatility. Too little swing in prices involves no trading opportunity; and too much removes the predictability of price trends.

3. *Timing of decisions.* Fundamental analysis is based on recent historical financial results—and this is a problem. The market is continually changing, moment to moment. Technicians correctly point out that fundamental analysis cannot be used for timing of trades. While the fundamentals can and should be used to pick stocks, you need to rely on technical signals for proper timing of buy and sell decisions. Swing trading is a valuable tool for this purpose.

Support and Resistance

The trading range of a stock is the price area in which that stock is being bought and sold. This range establishes what is "normal" so that when the stock's price moves above or below that range—or even when the price tests the edges of the range—those events are significant. In a nutshell, this is how technical analysis works. It is all about setting up and understanding a few rules, and then deciding what it means when the stock's price breaks those rules.

Trading range can take several different shapes. The most basic one is based on price, so that the trading range remains stationary. The top and bottom price do not change. A second type is the evolving trading range, in which the *spread* of the range remains approximately the same but the price edges upward or downward. These three types of trading ranges are illustrated in Figure 2.1.

When a trading range is evolving, technicians call this pattern *parallel price channels*, and are usually interpreted as foreshadowing a change in the trading range in the near future. The level and speed of an evolving trading range, a phenomenon called *momentum*, is also considered key in identifying how and when the trading range is going to adjust in the future.

spread
the point difference between high and low prices within a trading range; the larger the spread, the greater the price volatility.

Key Point

The trading range establishes the borders of what technicians consider normal for a stock. Any trading above or below that range offer a signal that important changes are about to occur.

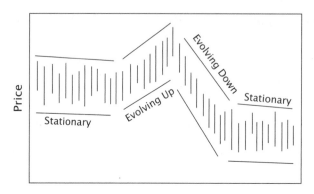

FIGURE 2.1   Trading Ranges

parallel price channels

the top and bottom edges of a trading range when price levels are evolving to the upside or downside, as opposed to a range in which prices remain stable within the range.

momentum

in technical analysis, the rate and speed of changes in price and trading range, believed to be a determining factor in how soon a trading pattern is likely to adjust.

The trading range is also defined by the all-important to and bottom price levels. As long as a stock remains within a defined trading range, these lines remain intact. But when price exceeds these price lines, that means that big changes are occurring and a new trading range is going to be established.

The top line of the trading range is called the *resistance* level. This is the highest price that traders are currently willing to pay for the stock. At the bottom is the *support* level, which is the lowest price that sellers will accept to relinquish stock. In the never-ending interaction between buyers and sellers, the support and resistance lines provide a definitive, price-based summary of the stock's current *supply and demand* levels.

Resistance and support are the foundations of technical analysis. They provide the standard by which a stock's performance is measured, in several respects. These standards include:

1. *The spread and thus the volatility of the stock.* The greater the swing in price from high to low within the trading range—the spread— the greater the volatility. High volatility is the most commonly used measure of market risk, so the technician will judge stock safety based on the spread itself.

Once the current trading change is violated and a new trend is set, a new trading range will be established for trading in the stock.

2. *The trend itself—flat, up or down.* The trend may be flat or evolving and this also helps to define the stock. Swing traders depend on a degree of volatility or the strategy simply will not work; most short-term traders will agree that they need some price swings in order to put their trading strategies in place. This is a short-term concern. A stock's price performance over the long term depends on the strength of the fundamentals for the company; short-term price performance is dominated by market emotions, and this is where moderate volatility is advantageous.

3. *The degree to which the trading range limits are tested and what those tests imply.* Technicians find themselves describing price movement as though the price itself were conscious. So they describe a price trend as "indecisive" or "aggressive." When the price approaches either resistance or support levels, technicians say that the price is "testing" those limits. A test that does not succeed is usually taken as a sign that price is about to make a move in the opposite direction; when the price does break through, that is taken as a significant development that throws the existing trading range into complete disarray and often leads to establishment of a new trading range. Many technicians like military analogies; so a

resistance

the highest price within a trading range, representing the top price that buyers are willing to pay for the stock under current conditions.

support

the lowest price within a trading range, representing the lowest price at which sellers will release their stock under current conditions.

supply and demand

the forces determining whether prices rise or fall. Increases in demand create upward price pressure, and increases in supply create downward price pressure; supply and demand are the causes of all stock price changes.

price breakthrough is described in the same way as a military breakthrough. It creates confusion and chaos and may lead to a disaster (or in the case of trading range, establishing a new "front line" for resistance or support).

4. *Actual changes in the trading range when price moves above or below established borders.* Once a breakthrough occurs, a period of volatility often follows, after which a new trading range is set. This is inevitable. Stock prices cannot be expected to remain within a narrow trading range indefinitely, so emerging changes in trading range and even in levels of volatility are part of a stock's life cycle. From the technicians' point of view, the changes are interpreted based on how the price settles down. The new trading range may be more volatile than the previous one, or less volatile. The previously stationary range may be replaced with an evolving one. The differences in price trend from one period to another are the interesting features of technical analysis. The unpredictability of price trends can be overcome, from a technical point of view, by accurately interpreting the signals.

5. *The implications when a stock is so volatile that a trading range cannot be established.* In some cases, a stock's price is behaving so erratically that no actual trading range can be established for the short term. The price is entirely unpredictable. This creates a problem for everyone because no technical interpretation is possible. The volatility is caused by some important uncertainty within the market, but instead of the price settling down to a flat short-term pattern, it becomes wildly unpredictable. This pattern is invariably short-term and caused by a passing problem or perception. An astute technical analyst knows that at such times, an examination of the underlying causes can help to estimate how long the high volatility is likely to last.

Key Point

Resistance and support are the defining attributes of a stock's price behavior. For swing traders, short-term trading is more important but the concepts of resistance and support provide important signals.

The study of resistance and support and the way that price acts within the trading range is important to swing traders because it helps you to anticipate likely price behavior in the next three to five days. While you are likely to depend on chart patterns and signals described in the next three chapters, always be aware of the trading range as well. It represents the price-based premise of a stock's risk level, price behavior, and future trends that have not yet developed fully.

The Advantage of Short-Term Chaos

Trading ranges bring a degree to order to an otherwise chaotic situation. No one knows what a stock's price is going to do next, just as no one can accurately predict the broader market. The auction marketplace in which stocks trade is unpredictable because there are so many competing forces and interests involved. An economic model discusses supply and demand as though buyers and sellers operated with single interests and motives. In practice, supply and demand is much different.

Because supply and demand are complex forces that interact on many different levels, prices never move in one direction indefinitely. When a stock's price rises, some owners will take profits and sell. The more shares that are sold, the more prices move downward. This interchange is continual. It also makes a difference when large *institutional investors* (such as mutual funds, insurance companies, and pension plan managers) buy or sell *blocks* of stock in a single move.

The individual investor, also known as the *retail investor*, accounts for only a small portion of total trading volume. This does not mean that individuals have no control in the market. Institutional investors tend to make the same errors as individuals; to trade on short-term emotion rather than logic; and to misread market signals. This is how you can use swing trading to your advantage. Institutions are too complex and have too many stocks in their portfolios to make fast decisions; as

institutional investors

large investors such as mutual funds, insurance companies or pension plans, holding diversified portfolios of stock and trading in blocks rather than only a few hundred shares. Institutional investors account for most of the market's treading volume.

blocks

large trades of stock executed by institutional investors in most cases, usually defined as 10,000 or more shares or stock with current value of $200,000 or more.

retail investor

an individual, in comparison to an institutional investor. The retail investor traditionally paid higher fees to trade, which explains the name. Today, any individual—even one paying low fees with a discount brokerage—is defined as a retail investor.

an individual, you can ride the waves of short-term price change and move in and out of positions rapidly.

Short-term chaos is the retail investor's advantage. Because your concern is for a small number of stocks and a very brief time window, you can make fast decisions and still pay minimal trading costs; and maximize your advantage as a swing trader. Because the short-term trend is always chaotic and dominated by greed, fear and uncertainty, you can expect one thing consistently: price is going to overreact to any and all news. So if a stock's earnings are a few cents below analysts' expectations, the stock may fall far more than the news justifies (only to adjust itself to a more reasonable level within a few days). This is a swing trading opportunity, of course.

You will also notice that the "chaos window"—the period of time when overreaction in either direction remains a controlling factor—lasts three to five days. This is why swing trading works well on that same schedule. It takes three to five days for buyers and sellers to recognize the overreaction in price and for the adjustment to get sorted out. In fact, the time institutional investors need just to correct their positions in a stock (represented by large blocks) makes it impossible for them to act any more rapidly. The disadvantage to institutional investors becomes the greatest advantage to individual swing traders.

In this respect, you can predict how prices will change in the short term. A distinction has to be made here between short-term price "trends" and longer-term market trends. The primary technical system in play in the market operates under the observations of the *Dow Theory*, developed by Dow Jones cofounder Charles Dow. Over a century ago,

Key Point

Investors desire predictability, but for swing traders, chaos creates opportunities. Chaos fuels greed, fear and uncertainly, and this fact is the swing trader's great advantage.

Dow realized that trends were the key to estimating future price movement. As his theories were fine-tuned over the years, the Dow Theory evolved into a series of rules and observations which are usually applied to the market as a whole and represented by the Dow Jones Industrials and other indexes.

The Dow Theory observes that a number of trends can be observed within the broader market. A long-term trend, once established by an index and then confirmed by another, establishes a market direction. However, short-term trends are discounted under the Dow Theory as unreliable.

This is true. If you are concerned with long-term trends for the entire market, you cannot rely on a two- to five-day price movement. More time is needed, and a longer-term primary or secondary trend has to be established. But swing traders are not concerned with these kinds of trends. The "trend" a swing trader follows is the short-term trend itself, which can be defined as the market's overreaction to virtually all news and all changes within the company and the individual stock. In this respect, swing traders observe the movements created by greed, fear and uncertainty, and make their decisions based on those momentary factors. You may pick stocks based on long-term growth and fundamental strength, but you trade on emotions, not fundamentals. This is where short-term chaos can be used to maximize your advantage.

> **Dow Theory**
> a major technical school of thought, a belief that overall market movement is predictable based on primary and secondary trends and confirming signals. The Dow Theory states that short-term trends are not reliable for predicting long-term price changes.

Breakouts from Trading Ranges

The short-term price movements within a trading range might be called insignificant. From a long-term point of view, this makes sense given the facts. Short-term trends cannot be relied upon to estimate long-term growth. Fundamental analysts will agree with this universally. Even technical analysts agree; but for swing trading, short-term price cycles are dominated by greed and by fear, and that is the key to swing trading success.

When prices shift in response to emotions, they are invariably exaggerated. So a greed-driven price increase will exceed any rational or justified growth in a stock's price; and fear-driven price declines will fall beyond a rational or justified level as well. In this regard, swing traders

---

Key Point

Greed and fear create over-reaction, thus exaggerated swings in both directions. By recognizing this tendency, swing traders profit from the tendencies of most investors. Remaining cool and collected leads to profits.

---

base their trades on emotions and not spend time analyzing the underlying causes for price movement. Those causes do not matter because price cycles are not reacting to any underlying cause; they are being driven by those emotions.

This is a very short-term shift in price. Swing traders may also be fundamental analysts and as long as you do not mix up the two different schools of thought, you can perform in both roles. But the time comes when price moves above resistance or below support. This can occur when the emotions of greed or fear are so exaggerated that a frenzy takes over, in which case it is likely that the price will eventually return to the established trading range. This is the exception; it is more likely that a *breakout* occurs because the stock price is on the way to establishing a new trading range.

A breakout occurs in many different variations, and following some specific charting patterns. Chartists rely on some of these patterns to predict a breakout. At times it is difficult to properly interpret a current chart pattern, but easier to identify in hindsight. Two breakout examples are provided in Figure 2.2.

A breakout can be more dramatic than the examples shown, with price levels moving far above or below established levels. A relatively low-volatility stock can become highly volatile for a period of time, only to settle down into a newly established trading range at a different level than previously. When you look at a long-range stock chart, you can spot the overall trends over many months or

breakout
a pattern in which price moves above resistance or below support and establishes a new trend and, eventually, a new trading range.

gap
a price pattern in which one day's opening price is higher than the previous day's highest price or lower than the previous day's lowest price.

Breakout Above Resistance

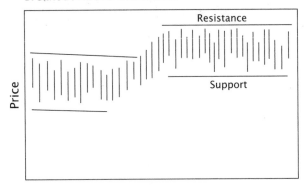

Breakout Below Support

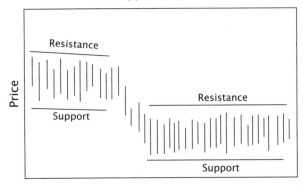

FIGURE 2.2 Breakout Above Resistance; Breakout Below Support

years, and this is where moving averages are valuable in identifying specific trends. But short-term changes in stock price levels can be very volatile, if only for a brief period of breakout and establishment of a new trading range.

Another significant trading pattern is the *gap*. As a general rule, stocks tend to open a new day within the high-low boundaries established on the previous day. The gap, also called the *common gap*, is not unusual. When a stock's price opens above the high point of the previous day or below its low point, a gap has occurred; and depending

common gap
another term for the gap, which distinguishes it from other forms of exceptional gap chart patterns.

breakaway gap

a gap involving price movement into new territory beyond the established trading range.

exhaustion gap

a type of gap in the direction of an extended price movement, signaling that the current trend is about to end and prices will level out or begin moving in the opposite direction.

runaway gap

a gap appearing as part of a strong and sustained price trend, reinforcing the price direction, and possibly showing up as a series of gaps one after another.

on the ensuing price activity, a gap may come in several different forms.

The *breakaway gap* involves price moving into a range where it has not been in the recent past, this is a "breakaway" from the previously established trading range. In comparison, the common gap takes place within an established trading range.

Two additional kinds of gaps are important to technicians. First is the *exhaustion gap*, which appears after an extended period of price movement upward or downward. While the exhaustion gap continues in the same direction, it signals that the price move may be coming to an end and the price trend will reverse. A *runaway gap* appears when a price movement is gaining in strength; this kind of gap reinforces the price direction, and a series of runaway gaps may even appear one after the other.

The major types of gaps are summarized in Figure 2.3.

Gaps are important to swing traders because of what they often signal. Gaps accompany major changes in directions occurring at the beginning of new price movements and also at the end of the same trends. If you watch charts and see patterns indicating the timing is right to make a trend, and form of confirmation strengthens your decision and improves your timing. Gaps serve as one of the best forms of confirmation to enter or exit a trade.

Key Point

Gaps are very important chart patterns because they invariably signal and reinforce important strength in existing trends, or foretell movement about to occur.

Common Gap

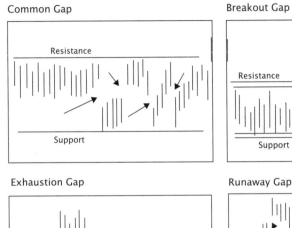

Breakout Gap

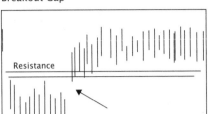

Exhaustion Gap

Runaway Gap

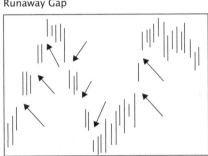

FIGURE 2.3 Common Gap, Breakout Gap, Exhaustion Gap, and Runaway Gap

Important Chart Patterns

As a swing trader you do not have to become an expert in all aspects of technical analysis—and some of it is quite complex. However, you do need to master the basic charting principles and these are relatively easy.

There are two general tiers to technical analysis. The largest and most complex is often overly theoretical and intensely mathematical. This level tends to be taught to students, and is more academic than practical. By the time you complete your analysis on this level, the stock has moved onto its next phase and the information is out of date. On a more immediate and accessible level are a few important basics. This is where you can quickly gain the knowledge you need to improve your timing and your profits with swing trading.

The best-known signals are patterns called *double top* and *double bottom* and these are fairly simple indicators to spot and to interpret. A double top involves two tests of resistance, with a decline in price in between. Because it is a double test, the double top is considered a bullish

double top

a price pattern in which resistance is tested twice with a pullback in between. As long as resistance holds up, price is expected to decline after the double top.

signal, and the stock price is expected to retreat. The concept here is that there was not enough enthusiasm among investors to push the price higher, so price retreats. The double bottom is the opposite, a test of support. Because support is strong enough to hold up under this two-part test, the price subsequently rises.

The double top and double bottom are illustrated in Figure 2.4.

Double Top

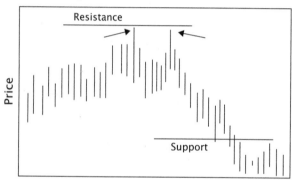

Double Bottom

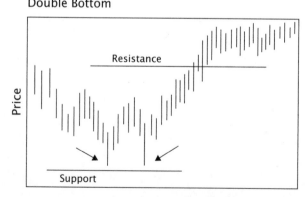

FIGURE 2.4 Double Top; Double Bottom

The head-and-shoulders pattern is an extended variation of the double top or bottom pattern. This is characterized by three price peaks or declines, with the middle one extending further than the first and third (in a letter M shape). A *head-and-shoulders top* occurs at or near resistance; the interim trading areas between the peaks is called the pattern's *neckline*. Volume often is strong at the first "shoulder," and relatively weak by the last phase of the pattern. The head-and-shoulders top is a test of resistance and because it does not break through, it anticipates a price decline.

The *head-and-shoulders bottom* tests support in the same way as the top tests resistance, but in the opposite pattern, in a letter W shape. Volume of the last of three head-and-shoulders extensions is likely to be lower than for the first shoulders and the inverse head, indicating a lack of enthusiasm among investors for a price decline. The head-and-shoulders bottom anticipates a rise in the stock's price.

The two head-and-shoulders patterns each anticipate price movement in the direction opposite of the tests; and may also anticipate breakouts from the established trading range (below support after the top pattern, or above resistance after the bottom pattern). Both of these are illustrated in Figure 2.5.

double bottom
a price pattern testing support with a price increase in between. Because support holds up against this two-part test, the double bottom anticipates a subsequent increase in the price level.

head-and-shoulders top
a price pattern with three peaks, the middle one higher than the first and third. This letter M shape pattern tests resistance and anticipates a price decline to follow.

neckline
the price area in between the price extremes of the head-and-shoulders pattern.

Key Point

The head and shoulders anticipates a reversal in price because it includes three separate tests of the limits, accompanied by weakening volume. The reduction in enthusiasm of investors is the real signal.

Top

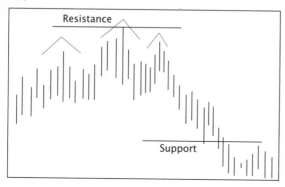

Bottom

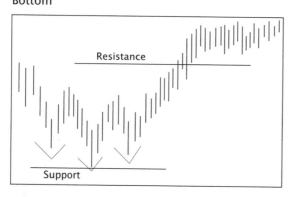

FIGURE 2.5   Head-and-shoulders Patterns Top and Bottom

head-and-shoulders bottom

the inverse of a top, consisting of a head testing support with two shorter shoulders before and after, creating a letter W shape. The pattern anticipates a price increase.

While the double top or bottom and head-and-shoulders patterns provide visual signals anticipating specific price trends, another important charting feature is the *broadening formation*. There is a tendency for price ranges to expand over time, often with accompanying expansion of daily volume. Several specific types of broadening formations are useful to swing traders to recognize patterns and to anticipate or confirm buy and sell signals.

The broadening formation is illustrated in Figure 2-6.

A related pattern is the *triangle*. This is the opposite of a broadening formation in which a trading range becomes narrower than the preceding pattern. This pattern implies uncertainty and what market watchers like to term "consolidation." But while it precedes some future price movement, it is difficult to determine with any consistency the direction that price movement is going to take.

The triangle is illustrated in Figure 2.7.

The triangle has been given other names such as "flags," "pennants," and "wedges," but the overall observation is the same: Any change to an existing trading range anticipates a future price direction. A broadening formation reveals the likelihood of stronger volatility in the future, and triangles imply momentary uncertainty.

No pattern can be reliably used to guarantee price movement. Even with the strongest of signals, short-term uncertainty dominates every stock's price. But these patterns, when incorporated into

broadening formations

chart patterns showing widening trading range for a stock, developing over time and providing specific signals for swing traders.

triangle

a price pattern in which the trading range narrows, a sign of uncertainty about the stock's price movement and a precursor of a coming upward or downward trend.

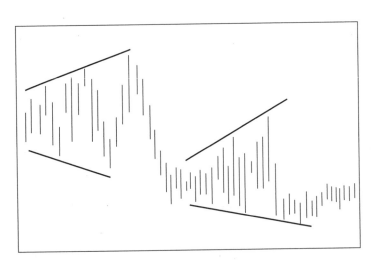

FIGURE 2.6 Broadening Formation

> ### Key Point
>
> The triangle pattern can be equated with uncertainty that often is found between periods dominated by greed and fear. For swing traders, this pattern can imply holding off any subsequent swing trade opening trades until that uncertainty gives way once more.

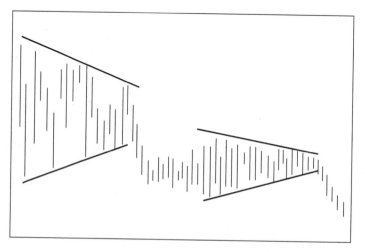

FIGURE 2.7   Triangle

the more specific daily price analysis used by swing traders, can serve as powerful confirmation tools. When these are used along with the additional information provided by candlestick charting analysis (discussed in Chapter 3), your arsenal of swing trading tools is vastly improved.

Spotting the Patterns to Trade Effectively

This brief explanation of charting patterns and signals is by no means exhaustive. Chart patterns are general indicators that may confirm other signals, and that is all. As you develop your swing trading strategy based on a day-to-day analysis of price trends, you will find the broader charting tools useful to time decisions. The purpose is to improve the timing and not to ensure 100 percent success. No system can do that.

It is always useful to keep market theories in mind. The random walk theory tells you that all short-term price movement is arbitrary. On the other extreme, the efficient market hypothesis claims that all current prices are fair because they reflect all known information about a stock. Neither of these theories is entirely reliable. They do, however, provide guidance to the market and promote an understanding of how and why prices move.

All theories aside, short-term price movement is always guided by greed, fear, and uncertainty. As a period of uncertainty becomes extended, a fourth emotion—impatience—is equally destructive as the other three. As long as you recognize that this range of emotions rules short-term price movement, you can employ swing trading to take advantage of the cyclical changes in a narrow window.

Some specific guidelines for using chart patterns within your swing trading strategy:

1. *Recognize the limitations of pattern analysis as well as the benefits.* Chart patterns are by no means the last word in timing of trades. Chart patterns may be thought of as the raw material of a more extensive timing strategy. As you will see in the next chapter, the day-to-day price trends contain their own specific formations and patterns that are not actually part of the broader chartist's realm. A chartist looks for longer-term patterns with double tops or bottoms, head and shoulders, and other visual patterns over an extended period of time; and gaps provide an indication of more rapid changes in the moment. But these trends are limited in value for swing trading. Because you will be observing trends from one day to the next, your concern is focused on the actual two- to five-day swings within a few points and based on price structure itself—and not so much on how the pattern fits into the larger chart pattern.

2. *Remember, price is not a conscious force.* There is a tendency among chartists to begin thinking about price and price movement as conscious forces. The names given to some patterns and the trends themselves are given descriptive names as well. Chartists refer to "testing support" or a price "trying to break through" resistance, as though it were a conscious effort. This may help in describing or understanding what is going on; but it is also important to recognize this as a trap. If you come to think

of price as having some type of free will, that facilitates the more deadly trap of acting on emotion and reacting to all price trends emotionally. Greed, fear and uncertainty rule most decision-making, but as a swing trader you will out-perform the market by remaining coldly detached and observing the short-term trends for the emotionally-driven cycles that they are.

3. *Don't depend on any one indicator; use many to confirm one another.* Every investor has a favorite indicator, either for stock selection of for timing of decisions. A lot of formulas are in use, and a lot of strategies that work once or twice might not work at all in the future. Cycles are notoriously unreliable and uncertain. For this reason, swing traders can and should use charting indicators and trends to confirm what they observe through a more detailed daily price cycle, and not as a stand-alone indicator. The more confirmation you have for what appears to be occurring in a stock's very short-term cycle, the better your timing is going to be. The value of chart analysis is that it is instantaneous and widely available free of charge. So you can either base your swing trading on candlestick charts and look to other kinds of charts for confirmation; or overlay the traditional chart patterns on the candlestick chart. In either form of analysis, your timing will improve when you base decisions on analysis and confirmation, and not on impulse.

4. *Learn how to recognize both patterns and false starts.* Perhaps the greatest challenge in charting is to know when a pattern is emerging and when a momentary change is only a false start. Looking back to last week's chart, you can easily identify the signals and see what you *should have done* at exactly the right moment. But if you look at the same chart today, what will happen next? The skill of chart reading relies not only on identification of a specific pattern, but also on being able to distinguish a genuine important signal from a false start. One fact is certain: Among all of the real signals are numerous false starts. Swing traders can use various chart patterns to minimize acting on false starts, but no one can eliminate them completely.

Charting is a key element to swing trading. In fact, the strategy depends on price patterns to work. But the traditional technical analysis and charting of a stock's price are only one form of analysis. The study of candlestick charts makes swing trading more effective than the traditional charting tools, and improves your timing immensely. The next chapter explores candlesticks in depth.

Candlestick Charting for Swing Trading

The method you select to track stock prices can make a big difference not only in timing of trades, but also in how you recognize opportunities. The traditional charting method showing the trading range and opening and closing prices is a valuable preliminary tool. For swing trading, however, you may want to expand your charting to include the *candlestick*.

The candlestick was originally developed hundreds of years ago in Japan to track rice futures, and in the late 20th century it became popular in the United States. One inhibiting factor before modern-day trading has been the problem of constructing a chart quickly. With the Internet, it is easy today to find free and instant charts for thousands of stocks. In the past, any service offering charting (of any kind) was invariably delayed and normally offered only for a fee. So with the Internet, candlestick charting has become a popular venue for stock price tracking, especially when used in conjunction with other methods (including moving averages and volume analysis).

candlestick
a chart formation showing each day's trading range; high and low price; opening and closing price; and the direction the price moved for the day. A white (or clear) candlestick reveals that the price closed higher than its open; and a black candlestick reflects a lower close for the day.

What the Candlestick Reveals

real body

in a candlestick chart, the rectangular central part. A white real body shows the stock moved up from opening to closing price. A black real body shows the stock moved down from opening to closing price.

As with all types of analysis, a single candlestick viewed by itself is of no value. You need to study the significance of a particular formation as part of a series; the tracking of candlesticks over several days is very revealing, especially in the way that formations appear—including not only the overall direction, but in whether the stock's daily prices move higher or lower, and for how long.

A candlestick consists of several parts; the two types of candlestick formations are summarized in Figure 3.1.

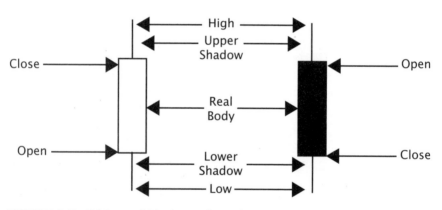

FIGURE 3.1 White and Black Candlesticks

Key Point

No system—candlesticks included—summarizing stock prices give you a sure-fire guarantee about the next move. But some indicators are more reliable than others.

The difference between these two candlesticks is in the *real body* itself. A white or clear real body—known as a *white candlestick*—reveals that the day's close was higher than the open—it was an up day. A black real body—a *black candlestick*—reveals the opposite: the close was lower than the open for the day.

The extensions above and below the real body are called *shadows*. The *upper shadow* is the trading range for the day between the real body and the high of the day. The *lower shadow* is the trading range between the real body and the low of the day.

The candlestick provides a wealth of information about a stock's trading for each day. The full extension from top to bottom is the day's entire trading range. The real body shows the distance between opening and closing price *and* also reveals whether the stock moved upward or downward on the day. These combinations of visual summaries become very important when candlesticks are studied as part of a trend on a stock chart.

Four variations on the usual candlestick formation—a real body with a shadow above and below—are important because they reveal important shifts or reversal points within trends. These four variations on the candlestick pattern are summarized in Figure 3.2.

white candlestick

a candlestick with a white or clear real body indicating that the stock moved up on the day.

black candlestick

a candlestick with a black real body showing that the stock moved down on the day.

shadow

in a candlestick, the area above and below the real body; the trading range above and below the opening and closing prices.

Key Point

The candlestick's main advantage is that it reports *everything* about a day's price movement, in a simple graphic form.

upper shadow

in a candlestick, the trading range between the day's high price and the top of the real body (opening or closing price).

lower shadow

in a candlestick, the trading range between the day's low price and the bottom of the real body (opening or closing price).

shaven head

a candlestick with no upper shadow and a white real body. This appears on a day when the stock rise and closed at its high of the day.

The *shaven head* is a candlestick with no upper shadow and a white real body. This formation has significance because it shows that the stock did not trade above its high for the day. The white real body shows that the stock rose in trading. As with all candlesticks, a particular outcome is important only to the degree that it fits into a trend and pattern; so it is not prudent to assign a particular meaning to this candlestick by itself.

The opposite of the shaven head is the *shaven bottom*. This shows up when a stock closes at its low for the day. It has no lower shadow and the real body is black.

The shaven candlesticks are illustrated in Figure 3.2.

A *spinning top* is a descriptive name given to candlesticks with small real bodies and the combination of a large upper shadow and a small lower shadow, indicating a broad trading range but minor gaps between opening and closing prices. These can occur in up as well as down markets. Examples are shown in Figure 3.3.

Shaven Head   Shaven Bottom

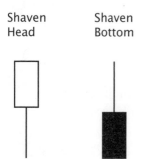

FIGURE 3.2   Shaven Candlesticks

Key Point

The imaginative names of candlesticks are useful in helping you to visualize not only the formation, but also its significance in a swing trading strategy.

Up Day   Down Day

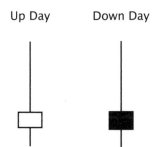

FIGURE 3.3 Spinning Tops

The *doji* is a candlestick with little or no real body. It is shaped like a cross, indicating that the space between opening and closing prices is very small, even though trading took place above and below. When this appears in a trend, it often signals that reversals are about to occur; so the doji is very important as part of a candlestick-based trend analysis. Swing traders may close attention to these narrow range days. Also called the *common doji*, it is distinguished from three other types.

Three other doji variations may be seen in candlestick charts. The first is the *long-legged doji*, which is unusual. When you see a very narrow space between opening and closing prices accompanied by a larger than normal trading range, it often indicates that the current trend is coming to an end.

The *gravestone doji* is a bullish formation. With little or no space between opening and closing prices, traders attempted to trade above those

shaven bottom

a candlestick with no lower shadow and a black real body; this appears on a day when the stock fell and closed at its low of the day.

spinning top

a candlestick with a large upper shadow and a small lower shadow and with a small real body that is either white or black.

doji

a candlestick with little or no real body, shaped like a cross. This demonstrates very little change between opening and closing prices, with trading occurring above and below those levels.

levels but were not successful. This often precedes a price retreat.

A final type of doji is the *dragonfly doji*, which is an opposite formation from the gravestone. With the dragonfly, there is little or no distance between opening and closing prices, but trading taking place on the day below that level. When this formation appears, it often precedes a price rise in the follow sessions.

These four types of doji formations are summarized in Figure 3.4.

Common

Long–legged

Gravestone

Dragonfly

FIGURE 3.4 Doji Candlesticks

The individual formations of candlestick trading are interesting and have descriptive names. However, for swing trading the two- to five-day trading patterns are far more revealing and important.

Patterns and Combinations

Candlesticks—as with all forms of trend analysis—have to be studied and interpreted as part of a trend. For this reason, swing traders *need* at least three consecutive days in order to decide which way a stock is heading, what is likely to come next, and when (and if) to take action.

Patterns are useful not only in what they tell you, but in what the lack of a specific pattern reveals. Impatience is a costly emotion in the market, but swing traders know that they have to wait for a clear signal before acting. While an active swing trading pattern normally extends from three to five days, there may be periods in which no clear patterns emerge at all. This is equally valuable to the clearest of signals. The *lack* of a signal tells you that it is not yet time to act.

Patterns consist of three or more emerging trends and, because swing trading is very short-term, you do not need to include long-term trends. The three or more days are enough to provide a signal.

In traditional chart analysis, traders look for double tops and bottoms, head and shoulders formations, and other *reversal signals*. Swing traders not only seek the same types of anticipation in their patterns; they need reversal signals to know when the short-term trend is likely to stop and begin moving in the opposite direction.

The candlestick reversal signals include many different formations, some very strong and others

common doji

another name for the doji, distinguished from other doji variations.

long-legged doji

a candlestick with little or no distance between opening and closing prices but exceptionally broad trading range above and below.

gravestone doji

a candlestick with little or no space between opening and closing price, but a trading range above those levels for the day.

dragonfly doji

a candlestick with little or no distance between opening and closing prices, but a trading range below that level for the day.

reversal signal

any chart pattern or trend implying that the current price direction is about to stop and begin moving in the opposite direction.

hammer

a candlestick pattern occurring at the end of a downtrend. It consists of a long lower shadow and a small real body, and signals a reversal and the start of an uptrend.

more subtle. The most basic among these are the *hammer* and the *hangman*. These are candlestick formations representing narrow range days. Both of these appear frequently at the top and the bottom of two- to five-day trends and are quite distinctive. The hammer has a long lower shadow combined with a small real body, which may be either white or black. The hammer shows up at the bottom of a downtrend and often signals that a new reversal—an uptrend—is about to begin. The hangman is the opposite; it appears at the top of an uptrend and may signal the beginning of a reversal and a downtrend. Like the hammer, the hangman also has a long lower shadow and may be white or black.

Figure 3.5 shows both of these formations as they occur at the end of existing trends.

Note that in this example both hammer and hangman were shown with black real bodies. In both of these formations, either a white or black real body will be found. An actual example of recurring hammer and hangman formations is shown in Figure 3.6 for Citicorp.

Hammer

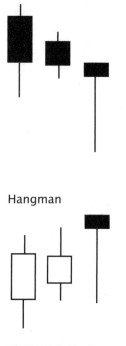

Hangman

FIGURE 3.5 Reversal Patterns

This chart reveals trading in June in a narrow range with several short-term trends. The notation A shows a hammer at the end of a brief, three-day price decline. The price rises over the following three days, ending at notation B, which is a hangman. The price does fall immediately after this day. Another brief uptrend occurs over three days ending with notation C, a second hangman, after which the price drops dramatically for four consecutive days.

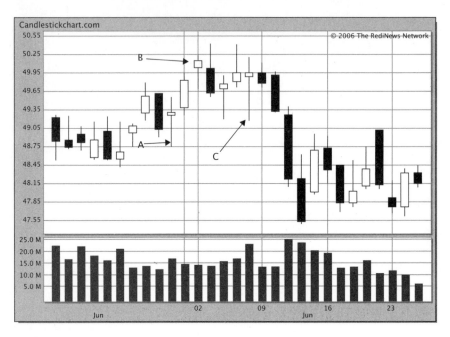

FIGURE 3.6 Hammer and Hangman Formations: Citigroup, Inc.

hangman

a candlestick pattern occurring at the end of an uptrend. It consists of a long lower shadow and a small real body and signals a reversal and the start of a downtrend.

The hangman and hammer will not always appear at the end of an uptrend or downtrend, but when it does the indicator can be quite strong. The typical swing trade strategy involves a multi-part series, and not just any one formation. The first is a series of three or more movements in one direction (with each day's closing higher than the opening in an uptrend, or lower than the opening in a downtrend). Second is the narrow range day which involves a very small real body. Typical of these formations are the hangman and the hammer. Third, and perhaps most important, is an initial trading day moving in the opposite direction. So, at the end of a downtrend, the formations are evident but followed by a move upward; and at the end of an uptrend, the narrow range day is followed by a move downward. Finally, the strongest possible signal is when the narrow range day is accompanied by exceptionally high volume. This is not essential to the timing of a swing trade, but it is certainly a strong form of confirmation that the trend is ending and about to move in the opposite direction.

These indicators are not consistent and this is what makes all analysis interesting. You need to develop the experience to interpret these patterns with and without confirmation, and to become well versed in formation reading.

Not every trend is going to look identical, either. There are times when trends change course without a hangman or hammer, or even a narrow range day. For example, one common pattern is the *engulfing line*. This occurs when the latest day's candlestick main body extends both above and below the previous day's, thus engulfing it. A *bullish engulfing line* has a white main body and a *bearish engulfing line* has a black main body.

Figure 3.7 provides examples of both bullish and bearish engulfing lines. The bullish engulfing line anticipates a rising trend in coming trading days, and the bearish engulfing line is the opposite; it anticipates falling prices in the stock.

To see the bullish engulfing line in an actual stock price history, refer to Figure 3.8. This is the candlestick chart for Microsoft. The arrow points to the bullish engulfing line, and over the course of the following four days, the stock rises. The fact that no engulfing line appears at the top of this uptrend makes an important point: The engulfing line formation is very revealing, but it does not always appear. In this case, a hanging man on the fourth day anticipates an extended downtrend in the stock.

engulfing line

a candlestick pattern in which the main body of a trading day extends higher *and* lower than the main body of the previous trading day.

bullish engulfing line

a candlestick engulfing line—one extending above and below the previous trading day's main body—with a white main body.

bearish engulfing line

a candlestick engulfing line—one extending above and below the previous trading day's main body—with a black main body.

Key Point

Engulfing lines occur often and may act as reliable signals of changing trend directions. While quite different than narrow range days—the opposite, in fact—the signals they provide can be given as much importance.

Bullish

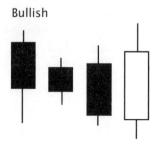

Bearish

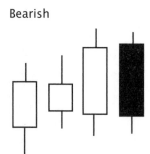

FIGURE 3.7 Bullish and Bearish Engulfing Lines

FIGURE 3.8 Candlestick Chart with Bullish Engulfing Line: Microsoft

A bearish engulfing line is shown for Ford Motor Company in Figure 3.9. Note that two bearish engulfing lines are shown with arrows. Both anticipate a downtrend. The first one is followed by four days moving swiftly downward. The second one is followed by four days of uncertainty and then one significant downward-moving day. Note that on the fourth day after the bearish engulfing line, a narrow range day precedes a large price drop. This may be thought of as a confirming signal. However, that day's trading closes higher rather than lower; so it is a mixed signal. You would expect the confirmation to point in the direction of the coming trend and in this case it does not. So with hindsight you may decide that more weight should be given to the bearish engulfing line than to the narrow range day; but without seeing the following day, these signals could also be confusing.

The confusing and contradictory pattern—a bearish engulfing line followed by a narrow range day that is white instead of black—is typical in periods of uncertainty. Buyers and sellers simply do not know which direction the price is going to move. Note that there are seven trading days of uncertainty in this example, preceded *and* followed by price declines. So the uncertainty merely interrupted the downtrend. This is the problem with periods of uncertainty. It is difficult to read, and swing

FIGURE 3.9 Candlestick Chart with Bearish Engulfing Lines: Ford Motor Company

---

Key Point

Signals may be followed by several days of uncertainty. This is why swing traders need not only the reversal signals, but a second signal indicating the new trend has begun.

---

traders often have to wait out the uncertainty before they can fully trust the charts. For example, once the uncertainty in this example ended, the stock declined dramatically, and then signaled a turn with a common doji and began an uptrend the following day.

The engulfing patterns demonstrate that the signals are very dependable, even when a brief period of uncertainty ensues. They do not always appear to provide a consistent signal, however, so the uncertainty itself is a type of signal telling you to wait. But when engulfing patterns do appear, the indication is very strong that a direction of specific movement (bullish or bearish) will soon follow.

Dozens of additional candlestick patterns can provide very good insights into stock movement. Combined with more traditional studies of trading range, support and resistance, and well-known reversal signals, the candlestick pattern is a valuable tool for every swing trader.

Valuable Resource

To find out more about candlestick patterns, check http://www.candlestickchart.com and link to both "bullish" and "bearish" patterns. This site provides visual descriptions as well as links for further explanation for more than 60 candlestick patterns. The site also provides cost-free candlestick charting services for thousands of stocks.

Similarities Between Opposite Candlestick Patterns

Any study of trading patterns is going to require experience. Many patterns look similar to one another but can be interpreted in different ways. Candlestick patterns are no exception.

For example, some bullish patterns might appear nearly the same as a bearish pattern, with entirely different outcomes. A bullish pattern called *concealing baby swallow* involves a series of black real bodies declining over several days. The first two days have no upper or lower shadow, a condition called *marubozu* in candlestick lingo. This pattern indicates that after reaching a new low, the trend will turn upward.

But a bearish pattern is nearly identical to concealing baby swallow. The *three black crows* pattern also consists of a series of black real bodies on the decline. A subtle difference is that in this pattern the three or more black real body days do have upper and lower shadows. The pattern implies that the market has been trading too high and is moving downward. But lacking a reversal pattern (such as a hammer) the three black crows is viewed as a bearish signal.

concealing baby swallow

a bullish candlestick pattern consisting of a series of four black real bodies in a declining trend, anticipating a reversal in coming trades.

marubozu

a candlestick with a real body but no upper or lower shadow; a day whose trading range is confined within opening and closing prices.

Key Point

Not every signal is obvious. Even with candlesticks, a pattern can have a bullish or a bearish interpretation. You need confirmation before making decisions based on only one aspect of price movement.

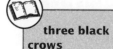

three black crows

a bearish candlestick pattern consisting of three or more black real body days in a downtrend.

These two patterns are illustrated in Figure 3.10.

The similarities of formation in these patterns make the point: While candlesticks are visually effective in chart interpretation, the similarities between some bullish and bearish patterns can lead to errors in timing or even in misreading the coming trend direction. With this in mind, it is important to combine candlestick analysis with traditional technical signals, *and* to seek the confirmation patterns indicating that reversals are about to occur. These include not only the apparent pattern as it develops, but also the narrow range day or engulfing line, and increased trading volume.

Concealing Baby Swallow (bullish)

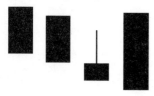

Three Black Crows (bearish)

FIGURE 3.10   Bullish and bearish candlesticks: Concealing Baby swallow and Three Black Crows

Key Point
It is a mistake to use any one form of analysis exclusively. Combining different forms—like traditional and candlestick charting—improves the overall quality of information and provides more confirmation.

Similarities can be found between many candlestick patterns, not just the one above. For example, the *three white soldiers* is a bullish pattern involving three long white days, each with a higher close than the previous; when this occurs within a broader downtrend, it indicates a change and reversal. Another pattern called *deliberation* is bearish, although it looks very much like three white soldiers. In deliberation, a gap occurs between the two latest days and this pattern occurs at the end of an uptrend, signaling the end and a coming reversal. So, even when patterns are very similar, their significance depends on what kind of trend is underway before the formation; and on often subtle differences in the actual formation.

These two candlestick patterns are summarized in Figure 3.11.

The obvious similarities between many candlestick patterns only reinforce the importance of multi-level analysis and confirmation. It is too easy for traders to misread signals, only to recognize their error in hindsight. This problem is not limited to swing traders; all technicians and chartists suffer from the same tendency to misread a signal.

three white soldiers
a bullish candlestick occurring at the end of a downtrend, consisting of three or more consecutive white real bodies closing higher on each day.

deliberation
a bearish candlestick appearing within an uptrend, involving three consecutive white real bodies closing higher than the previous day, with the final day opening with a gap above the previous close.

Bullish and Bearish Candlesticks

Three White Soldiers (bullish)

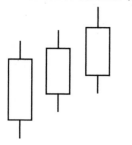

Deliberation (bearish)

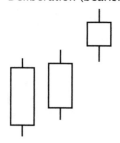

FIGURE 3.11   Bullish and Bearish Candlesticks: Three White Soldiers and Deliberation

You can never achieve 100 percent accuracy in the interpretation of trends or in the timing of trades; but using confirmation and a variety of technical analytical tools you can improve your odds. A good rule of thumb is that whenever a pattern is uncertain, it makes sense to *not* enter into a transaction. The lack of a clear indicator should act as a warning sign. Even when you are confident that you are reading signals accurately, there are no guarantees. But the many tools available through traditional technical analysis and the use of candlestick charting can improve the percentages in your favor.

Key Point

If you find yourself misreading signals, you're not alone. Everyone, even the most experienced chartists, never have foresight as good as their hindsight.

Sources of Cost-Free Charts

Many websites offer cost-free charting services. Normally, these services include the combination of OHLC pricing with 200-day moving averages or volume. You can find free charts on most sites by entering a stock's symbol and seeking a quote; the chart accompanies the quote. For example, the following services all provide free quotes and charts:

Bloomberg	www.bloomberg.com
CNN	money.cnn.com
Yahoo Finance	finance.yahoo.com
MSN Money	moneycentral.msn.com
Forbes	www.forbes.com

All online brokerage services also provide free charting to their clients. The most popular discount brokerage services include:

Charles Schwab	www.schwab.com
e*trade	www.etrade.com
Scott Trade	www.scottrade.com
TD Ameritrade	www.tdameritrade.com

For free candlestick charting with moving averages and volume, check the website *http://stockcharts.com/index.html*. This site is useful because of the combined information it provides.

For a thorough explanation of charting, free charts, and visual summaries of all chart patterns, the best free site is *http://www.candlestickchart.com*. The site's free services include candlestick charting with volume for any stock as well as descriptions of bullish and bearish candlestick patterns. Subscribers get advanced charting service and support. The highly visual, cost-free charting and tutorials make this a valuable tool for swing traders.

The whole key to swing trading is recognition of the patterns as they emerge. The candlestick chart is one of the best ways to study short-term trends in price. Recognizing when price movement occurs as part of a reaction cycle is equally important. This is the topic of the next chapter.

Chapter 4

Reaction Swings and the Reaction Cycle

Even though short-term price trends appear random, there are methods for identifying turning points. That means finding those price moments where the short-term cycle is likely to begin swinging in the opposite direction.

The two- to five-day price trends swing traders use are part of a highly chaotic system. Buyers and sellers trade off control over price—and only for those few days of cyclical change. When buyers are in control, prices rise. However, once the price becomes high enough—often only by points or fractions of points—selling pressure increases and the sellers take over. These fast-moving and frequent turns are *reaction swings*, the times in short-term price change when direction is reversed. These changes occur due to the immediate and short-term exchange of control between buyers and sellers.

> **reaction swings**
> short-term changes in price trend resulting from the reaction of buyers to sellers and vice versa.

Newton's Third Law observes that each action has an equal and opposite reaction, and market pricing follows the same rule. When buying pressure forces prices upward, that results in selling pressure that takes over and pushes prices down. This continues in the swing trader's two- to five-day cycle. Buyers and sellers operate in this situation as "action/reaction force

---

Key Point

Just as physics dictates how objects interact, the natural cycles of price dictate action and reaction.

---

pairs," which in physics describes what occurs when objects meet. For example, when a hammer strikes a nail, the nail goes into the wood, but some offsetting bounce moves back into the hammer. This force pair is easily noticed by direct action. The interaction of buyers and sellers is more subtle—and the more you study price charts, the more you actually begin to see the reaction cycle in action.

The engulfing line and narrow range day patterns you see in candlesticks are symptoms of the interaction between buyer and seller. They represent the price equivalent of a nail moving through wood, the noise the hammer makes on the nail, and the offsetting reverberation. In the candlestick chart, the narrow range day indicates that the current trend is reaching its exhaustion point and that, once the price direction moves away from that trend, the price cycle is about to move in the opposite direction—the force pair at work. An opposite version of the same idea is the engulfing line, which involves an expanded trading range—but with open or close in the opposite direction. In this reaction swing, the exhaustion is hidden within the two days' candlesticks (the last day of the existing trend and the day of the engulfing line); and the reversal of patterns is quickly established. So a downtrend (characterized by a series of black real-body days) ends with an engulfing line pattern and a white real body, the beginning of an upward reversal swing; and an uptrend (characterized by a series of white real bodies) ends when an engulfing line pattern follows with a black real body.

Both of these reversal patterns tell you the reaction swing is likely to be underway. An important point to make here concerns the *direction* of price movement. The swing trader does not care whether prices move up or down. You know that the two- to five-day window is an opportunity to trade a stock and to make a short-term profit. Swing trading works in both directions.

Stock investors tend to be overly optimistic and are focused on upswings only. So the tendency is to look for the end of downswings, with the idea of buying at the low and then selling at the end of the upswing. This, however, is only one of two methods for getting in and out of the market. By emphasizing only the upswing, you would miss half of the swing trading opportunities. Remember, reaction swings happen in both directions with consistency. By recognizing that both up and down price movements are opportunities, you double your chances for swing trading profits.

Studying Action and Reaction of Stocks

As a swing trader, you look for and identify specific patterns indicating change in direction. This swing occurs predictably, but it is not the same as momentum. A reaction swing is just that: a reaction by sellers to buyers' recent action, and on the other end of the swing, a reaction by buyers to sellers' recent action. This is not the same as momentum, and recognizing the differences in the patterns help you to avoid making your move at the wrong time.

Patterns emerge for both swings and momentum and they are not the same. In a swing pattern, a few specific signs occur. These include three primary signals:

1. *The swing trading cycle.* This involves three or more days in which specific repetitive patterns emerge. In an uptrend, you expect to see a series of higher highs, offset by a responsive series of higher lows. In a downtrend, you expect to see a series of lower lows offset by lower highs. The uptrend and downtrend patterns are illustrated in Figure 4.1 and Figure 4.2 respectively.

Key Point

Swing in price is not the same a spice momentum. While swing moves back and forth, momentum is a strong move in one direction.

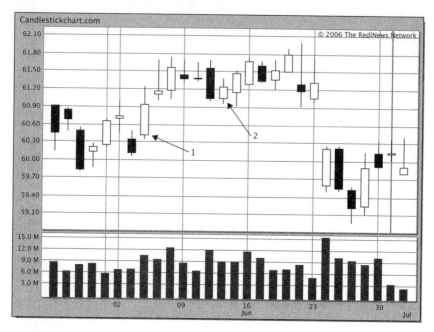

FIGURE 4.1 Uptrend: Johnson and Johnson

Source: Candlestickchart.com.

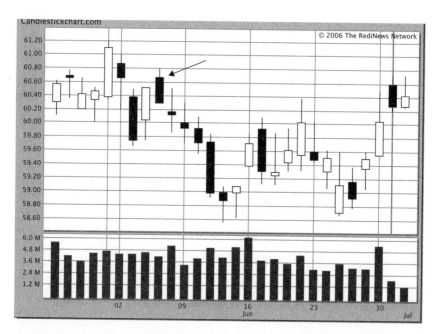

FIGURE 4.2 Downtrend: Pepsi Cola

Source: Candlestickchart.com.

The uptrend on Figure 4.1 for Johnson and Johnson appears in two places. The beginning of these trends are marked 1 and 2. In both cases, there are a series of higher highs offset by a series of higher lows.

The downtrend on Figure 4.2 for Pepsi Cola has six periods, an exceptionally long and sustained series of lower lows offset by lower highs; but this meets the criteria. Note that the series ends with a narrow range day and the immediate beginning of an uptrend.

2. *The narrow range day or engulfing line.* The *end* of the uptrend or downtrend is signaled in one of two ways. The narrow range day has two components. First is the narrow range itself, and second is a movement in the opposite direction. On Figure 4.2, the strong downtrend in Pepsi Cola stock extends over six days and ends with a narrow range day with the stock moving higher instead of lower. This is a strong signal and subsequent trading showed that the signal was correct.

> ### Key Point
>
> The engulfing line is an alternative signal that a trend may be re-versing, especially when accompanied with high volume. But if volume is not high, the engulfing line may provide a false signal.

The engulfing line is equally as strong but often difficult to read. At times you will get a false signal by depending on the engulfing line alone, so it makes sense to wait for one additional trading day before making your move. For example, Figure 4.1 shows a large price gap and decline following a bullish engulfing line. Two important points should be made about this false signal. First, it appears at the conclusion of five days of uncertainty, so you really have no way to know how the stock is going to move next. Second, the engulfing line is accompanied by exceptionally *low* volume. In order to proceed with confidence at the end of a trend, you expect to see higher than average volume.

3. *High volume on a narrow range day.* The narrow range day by it-self is a promising indicator that the end is over. But when vol-ume is also high, that is a very strong signal confirming the end of the trend. The combination of a narrow range day with high volume is illustrated in Figure 4.3.

In this example, Blockbuster demonstrated two end-of-trend com-binations of a narrow range day and higher than average volume. These points are indicated as 1 and 2 on the figure. The first shows steam run-ning out of an uptrend and is a large spinning top (large trading range with narrow real body); and it is followed by a downtrend. Volume for the narrow range day was also exceptionally high.

> ### Key Point
>
> When you see both a narrow range day *and* exceptionally high volume, that is the strongest sign of all that the current trend is about to turn. If, on the next trading day, the stock moves in the opposite direction, it is almost always enough confirmation.

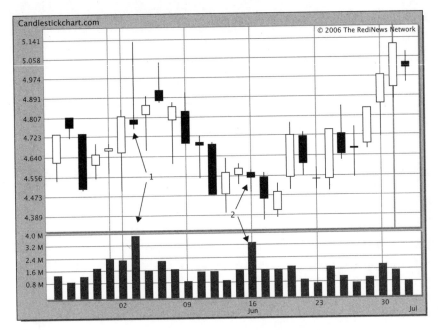

FIGURE 4.3 Narrow Range Day with High Volume: Blockbuster

Source: Candlestickchart.com.

In the second example, the narrow range day was also accompanied by high volume, but the other signals were not clear; the end of the downtrend actually came two days later, and was followed by a strong and sustained uptrend. In both examples, the high-volume days were key turning points even though the reversals were delayed by two trading periods.

In comparison to the swing trading buy and sell signals, momentum is far different. It is characterized by sustained periods of movement in a single direction, lacking any patterns indicating the end of the trend. An example of a stock demonstrating first a downward momentum and then upward momentum, is shown in Figure 4.4.

In this example, Microsoft Corporation's stock experienced downward momentum over 12 sessions followed immediately by upward momentum for seven sessions. The lack of any reversal signals during these periods demonstrates the difference between swing trading and momentum trading. The only reversal in this two-part pattern of momentum occurred at the end of the downturn, where the classic three-day pattern occurred (three days of lower lows, offset with lower highs). Yet no confirming patterns (narrow range days or engulfing lines) occurred—another sign that these were periods of momentum and not swings.

Key Point

When you see continued trends without reversal signals, or weak reversal signs lacking confirmation, it probably means you are seeing momentum and not swing.

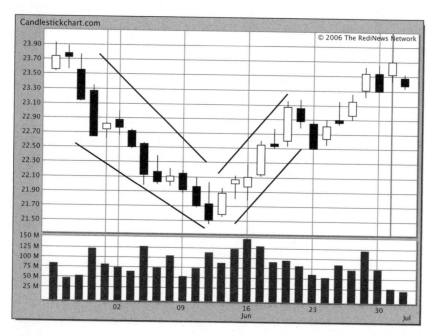

FIGURE 4.4 Downward Momentum and Upward Momentum: Microsoft Corporation

Source: Candlestickchart.com.

The typical swing trade involves repetitive and easily identified patterns. Momentum trading disrupts this pattern and swing traders cannot accurately judge the duration or extent of momentum. They can only wait out the momentum period and look for a return to the more typical swing trading cycles.

Experience provides you with the ability to combine technical charting analysis with swing trading to (1) distinguish between swings and momentum; (2) use both in combination to recognize developing patterns; and (3) avoid making mistakes resulting from nonrecognition of emerging longer-term trends. The direction and size of the trading range are key technical indicators. Swing traders are interested in the short-term changes in price, of course, but should also be aware of the longer-term trend within the trading *channel* of a stock.

channel

the overall direction of a stock's price movement; the trend, which may be flat, upward, or downward over many months.

A channel may be flat, meaning that price does not move upward or downward over a period of time, except for small swings within a confined trading range. In some respects, a *flat channel* can represent the best swing trading opportunity because short-term price change occurs without a longer-term trend of more dynamic change. An *ascending channel* shows that, even given short-term price swings, the longer-term trend of the stock is clearly upward. An example is provided in Figure 4.5

The example of the Charles Schwab Corporation shows that the channel moved upward for

flat channel

a channel whose trading range remains the same over time, with neither rising or falling price trend exhibited for a period of months.

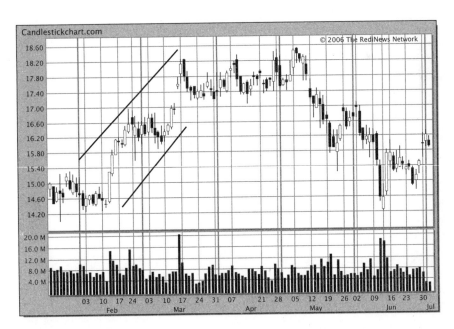

FIGURE 4.5 Ascending Channel: Charles Schwab Corporation
Source: Candlestickchart.com.

Key Point

The direction of the channel gives you a good idea of the longer-term trend. You will still experience swings within the overall channel direction.

ascending channel

a channel with a rising trading range over time. Short-term swings in price occur, but the longer-term price trend is upward.

about one-third of the 120-day period shown in this chart. This was followed by approximately equal-length uncertainty and then a downtrending channel.

A *descending channel* is the opposite, a trading range with swings occurring within trading range but longer-term trend toward downward price movement. An example is provided in Figure 4.6.

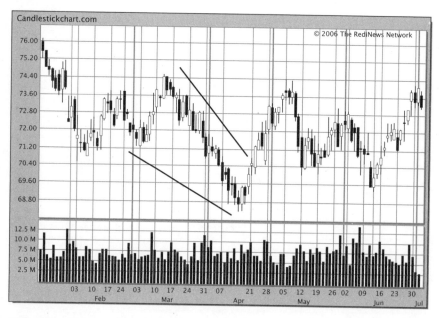

FIGURE 4.6 Descending Channel: Altria Corporation
Source: Candlestickchart.com.

The example of Altria Corporation's 120-day chart showed a downtrend in the first portion. Here the swings occurred within a declining trading range. The swing trader who is aware of the longer-term direction of the price channel will be better equipped to select stocks for swing trading and to recognize when channel trading trends are coming to a close. The channel pattern is revealing because, when it ends, a period of long-term uncertainty is likely to follow. For the swing trader, this new period requires caution while also presenting new swing trading opportunities.

descending channel
a trading range moving downward in price over a period of months.

Price and Volume Spikes

In the course of studying charts, you will notice that price movement is rarely consistent or steady, even in the middle of strong trends. At times you will also see aberrations in price movement. These *spikes* moving above or below the established pattern may occur at any time and, lacking confirming indicators of big change, may not be important. However, when a spike is accompanied by exceptionally high volume, preceding price gaps, or external influences (such as pending mergers, earnings surprises, or change in management, for example), it may not be an exception but a *power spike*.

spike
an unusual price movement, above or below established trading range, and often followed by a return to that range.

When spikes occur for no apparent reason and the trading range is immediately reestablished, it can be ignored—assuming that nothing else in the price pattern occurs—because it may not hold exceptional importance. When viewed as part of a longer-term trend, the spike may have no charting importance. For the swing trader, a spike of this type can be ignored. Remember, swing traders are involved with two- to five-day periods and not with longer-term trends. Of course, if those longer-term trends are going to affect the channel direction of the stock, then the spike cannot be ignored.

power spike
a price spike above or below trading range accompanied by unusually high volume or other price patterns and signaling a change in the chart pattern.

An example of a stock with two spikes is shown in Figure 4.7.

Key Point

A spike occurring by itself, followed by a return to the established trading range, may be ignored as having no permanent significance for swing trading.

In this 120-day chart, Hormel Foods had two spikes. The first, marked 1, was accompanied with exceptionally heavy volume. Note that the spike in this case was a shadow and not part of the real body of the candlestick; the day's price movement was downward. This is a classic example of an attempt on the part of buyers to take the price higher, but that attempt failed. This power spike resulted in a three-week bearish trend, ending with the second of the two spikes, marked on the chart as 2.

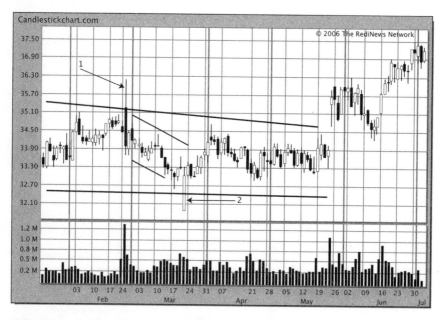

FIGURE 4.7   Stock with Two Spikes: Hormel Foods

Source: Candlestickchart.com.

Key Point

When a spike is accompanied with heavy volume on the same day, it is probably a power spike. This anticipates price movement and trading range adjustments.

In the second spike, you can see several notable differences. First, the volume level is not different than surrounding days. Second, the downward spike is part of a real body. Third, the day's price closed up. This spike appears to hold no special characteristics like the first one did. The most compelling evidence of this is that price levels returned to the established range, which is marked and extends over four months.

Candlestick chartists look for a relationship between price spikes and breakouts. This more typical power spike may signal a significant change in trading range and for swing traders the signal also provides a strong signal to make a move. Some such moves may be quite dramatic. When you study the power spike in the context of a traditional swing trading setup (three or more days in a trend, for example), the signal with the power spike may be very strong, either on the side of entering or leaving the position.

An example of a power spike is shown in Figure 4.8.

In this chart, the price for Alberto-Culver spiked dramatically with a long upper shadow. This day also say extremely high volume. To the swing trader, the problem with such an unusual formation is that it does not give a clear signal. However, the high volume and the downward-moving day offer a hint. The following three sessions do establish the traditional three-day downtrend pattern. This ends with a bullish engulfing line, which is followed by a sustained and very strong uptrend. In this example, the upper shadow spike is the first hint of a coming downtrend. Buyers were not successful in forcing the price higher on the spike day; and a following three-day downtrend ends up with a clear buy signal for the swing trader.

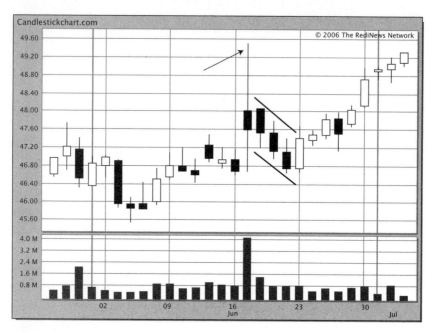

FIGURE 4.8 Power Spike: Alberto-Culver
Source: Candlestickchart.com.

Power spikes may precede such movements and, in this instance, a brief downtrend was followed by a strong uptrend. The pattern involves two distinct signals working together. The spike itself was a power spike in the sense that volume was quite heavy. The fact that the spike occurred in the shadow only and not within the day's opening and closing prices is not as compelling as one with a real body, but it is a power spike nonetheless. The following sessions are a response to the unsuccessful attempt to push prices higher, but once that three-day downtrend ended, a strong uptrend followed. The end of the downtrend was the second of the two swing trade signals.

Managing the Reaction Swing

The typical swing occurs as part of the normal trading cycle, the interaction between buyers and sellers. It reflects the never-ending greed/fear emotional mindset that dominates short-term trading, and is a continual adjustment of price perception on both sides. Swing trading occurs naturally as part of this never-ending swing pattern.

This action/reaction (the reaction swing) occurs as a series of price corrections within a larger, longer-term trend. The various patterns technical analysts use in chart study—such as triangles, wedges, flags, and pennants—all are part of this correction trending. They help you to predict how and when direction of price is going to change. The trick is in the timing.

Swing trading and the prediction process must involve the count of trading cycles. This is why emphasis is placed on the typical two- to five-day period. This is where swing trades usually occur. In a continuation of a strong trend, you can go along for the ride of a trend when the maximum five days are exceeded. Figure 4.8 provides an example of such an opportunity. Following a two-part signal (upper shadow spike with high volume, and classic three-day downtrend ending with an engulfing line) the buy signal could not have been stronger. At the low point, the swing trader knew it was time to buy. Yet instead of a two-to five-day cycle, the ensuing uptrend extended at least eight days and possibly more. The interesting point in this pattern was that, lacking any reversal signal (in price, volume spikes, or bearish price gaps), the swing trader would be likely to hold on through the entire upswing, no matter how long it would last.

The series of three periods occurs so frequently that swing traders can find themselves making decisions on false signals prematurely. Figure 4.8 contains a good example of this. If you look at the strong uptrend following the spike and downtrend, after three uptrend days, the stock showed one black real body. It was not an engulfing line, a narrow range day, or a high-volume day. Even so, it did follow three uptrend days, so some swing traders would take profits at that point and sell. The problem with this is that there is not a sell signal. If a swing trader is going to react to a three-day trend, then there are plenty of pitfalls along the day. It leads to poor timing. This is why the reaction swing *requires* a signal of the price moving in the opposite direction. So either the narrow range day or an engulfing line is essential to the timing of swing trades. Without one of these, you really cannot know whether the short-term trend is over or will continue.

The problem swing traders face is distinguishing between the two-to five-day trend and actual momentum. With momentum, you need to wait out the exhaustion of the trend, even though it may move beyond the two-to five-day window. Figure 4.8 demonstrates this in the strong uptrend at the conclusion of the chart. To its very end there exists no signal that momentum is over. In fact, the two price gaps in the trading periods four and five days prior to the chart's end give strong evidence that the trend will continue. This runaway gap moves the stock above the established trading range (not counting the spike) and continues the uptrend.

Swing traders cannot rely on repetitive and consistent patterns, as this example demonstrates. In fact, the power spike may precede momentum, even when that momentum runs in an opposite direction. The uncertainty of how price moves after a power spike serves as a warning as well as an opportunity. For example, given the failure of Alberto-Culver buyers to move the stock into higher territory on the day of the spike, it would be reasonable to conclude that the stock would move downward. It did, but only for three days. If momentum were to occur after the spike, it stands to reason that, failing the attempt to move price higher, that momentum would be downward. The typical swing trade pattern of three down days ending with a bullish engulfing line contradicted this, however, and the momentum move was up. In this case, the spike was only a first attempt; ultimately, buyers did prevail and the price did move up beyond established trading range.

> **Key Point**
>
> A power spike can be interpreted in more than one way. A cautious trader may want to wait and see which direction prices will move before entering a post-spike trade.

In managing the reaction swing, you may seek further types of signaling events. The obvious ones are clear: three or more days of specific trends are always necessary (higher highs and higher lows indicating an uptrend, and lower lows with lower highs indicating a downtrend). In addition, you need to identify strongly confirming signals, of which there are three common types. These are the narrow range day, higher than average volume, or the engulfing line. When higher than average volume accompanies either the narrow range day or the engulfing line, it is the strongest possible type of confirmation.

There are additional confirming signals. On the upside, when a stock reaches a *new high*, for example, that may confirm the end of a recent uptrend as part of a swing trade timing strategy. A new high is usually defined as a high price for the past 52 weeks and, while such an occurrence is unlikely to show up frequently, it may be used as confirmation that a current swing trade is about to be exhausted.

new high
the highest price a stock has reached during the past 52 weeks.

A *new low* is the equivalent confirming signal at the end of a swing trading downtrend. Once sellers have driven prices down to a record one-year level, it is more likely than ever that a reaction swing will occur.

new low
the lowest price a stock has reached during the past 52 weeks.

However, because swing traders are less interested in long-term trends and more intent on short-term price changes, confirmation does not need to take the form of a 52-week record. When a stock has been trading in a narrowly defined trading range, and breakout above or below that level will establish immediate record high or low levels based on

---

Key Point

The analysis of new high and new low prices does not have to be based on 52 weeks. It may make more sense to study price changes based on the existing trading range rather than on a time constraint.

---

the established range. In fact, the breakout new high or new low may provide stronger immediate confirmation than a one-year record. If, for example, a stock has been hovering within a three-point range for nine months, and inches slightly above or below that narrow range, how significant is the change? For swing trading purposes, it may be more important to observe a stock cycling within three points for a month, and suddenly jumping above or below that shorter-term trading range—not for long-term investing purposes, for solely for swing trading confirmation.

The End of the Reaction Swing

A lot of focus is placed on finding the beginning of the reaction swing, but the ending is equally important. Successful timing of your entry is only half the equation; you also need to know when to get out.

The end of a reaction swing is often the beginning of a new one. So many swing traders will follow the closing of a transaction with an opposite buy (buy-sell followed by sell-buy; or the reverse sequence, sell-buy followed with a buy-sell).

There is often a one- to two-day pause between swings, which may be a brief period of uncertainty (or even a longer one), or the time you need to verify and confirm the signal. The narrow range day with high volume may be enough to prompt you to close out an existing swing trade position. But you may not want to open a new one until you see a following day occurring in the opposite direction.

You may also begin to recognize repetitive signals within your swing trading cycles. Uptrends may end with a similar signal over and over and downtrends end with a different but recurring signal as shown in Figure 4.9.

FIGURE 4.9 Repetitive Signals: Federal Express

Source: Candlestickchart.com.

This is a 90-day chart for Federal Express. There are six points emphasized. Points 1, 3 and 5 are all bearish engulfing lines that signal the end of uptrends. Points 2, 4 and 6 are all narrow range days signaling the end of swing trading downtrends.

You may also note a consistency in the duration of these uptrends and downtrends, which is by no means assured. However, for as long as the duration remains consistent, swing trading can be more accurately timed. Be aware, however, that no pattern or series of patterns lasts forever. All stock pricing trends alternate between periods of high action

Key Point

Some recurring patterns can provide strong confirmation for swing trading. But remember, these are never permanent. Cycles are continually evolving and changing.

and relative quiet. Swing traders emphasize the action/reaction with an awareness of the role played by greed, fear and uncertainty; and time decisions based on a study of the signals within the price pattern itself.

The consistency in trading like that for Federal Express shown in Figure 4.9 lasted about two months. However, followed that trend, the stock broke from its cyclical pattern and began an uptrend for the subsequent two months. This is not at all unusual. A period of predictable upswing and downswing patterns complete with signals (bearish engulfing lines at the top and narrow range days at the bottom) led to an extended period of upward price momentum. Here again, you will note the complete absence of a swing trading sell signal with confirmation after point 6. This makes the point that nothing remains unchanged forever and also that a period of predictable cycles may be followed by either a time of flat price and uncertainty, *or* by a period of strong momentum in either direction.

Because every reaction swing is likely to end differently, you need to set rules for yourself concerning the entry and exit of a trade. Three rules are recommended for every swing trader:

1. *Enter trades only when the signals appear and are confirmed.* Impatience may be called the fourth emotion of the market, and is worth resisting. You need confirmation to enter the trade. After a three-day or more period of specific trend, you should wait for the narrow range day or the engulfing line.

2. *Exit trades based on a predetermined criterion.* Your timing of exit is not quite as critical as timing for the entry. For example, you may exit without confirmation as long as you want to take profits and then go to the sidelines to await the next entry signal with confirmation. However, you may also apply the same rule on exit as you use for entry, requiring confirmation of an exit signal. This assures that an extended trend may be ridden for many periods beyond the two- to five-day "normal" swing trading period. You may experience some losses because you didn't take profits when you could have; but the decision should be based on your experiences and observations.

3. *Use trailing stops to protect long position profits.* If you want to lock in incremental profits while continuing to ride trends, use the *trailing stop.* This is a type of order which establishes a percentage level below market price, which is adjusted as the price changes. This type of order automatically triggers a sale if the stock's price begins to fall.

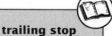

trailing stop

a trading order that sets a percentage below current price. If and when the stock falls to that price or below, a sale is generated automatically.

For short positions or to trigger an entry, swing traders can also use a *buy stop* order. This order generates an automatic buy when the stock moves up to a specified target price. This can either open a transaction or cut losses when your position is short.

buy stop

a type of order that generates an automate buy if and when the stock moves to or above a specified price.

Any swing trader knows that no pattern is going to repeat itself consistently. Even when repetitive cycles continue for several weeks or even months, the timing of the reaction cycle is never certain. Even those who try to depend on timing assumptions discover that the swing trade setup is the only dependable indicator to use. The two- to five-day period is common for most short-term trades. Swing traders rely on a multiple-day trend, confirmed by a narrow range day or an engulfing line. And for very strong confirmation, exceptionally high volume is also an excellent indicator that the reaction cycle is about to move in the opposite direction.

The next chapter explains a further restriction on swing trading: the brokerage rules and requirements and regulations about high-activity trading.

5

Brokerage Rules and the Pattern Day Trader

Every online brokerage service imposes its own set of rules. These rules are dictated by federal law and overseen by the Securities and Exchange Commission (SEC) as well as by the industry's self-regulatory body, the National Association of Securities Dealers (NASD) and the Federal Reserve Board.

The rules governing actions of listed corporations, their executives and boards, auditing firms, analysts, brokers and investors are complex. For swing traders, a handful of specific rules and the details of how orders get placed are of great importance. In fact, there may be a built-in conflict between any form of automatic order placement and the ideal timing of swing trades. An automatic order results in execution when specific circumstances are met (usually a specified price level). But it is possible for price levels to be met without the swing trade setup or execution pattern.

Specialized orders are useful to limit losses or to take profits at a predetermined level. When orders are placed using programmed limits or closing criteria, you modify the swing trading system to cut losses, take profits, or to close out the swing trade when predetermined events unfold.

Valuable Resource

To find out more about the regulatory agencies for the securities business, go to the SEC website at *http://www.sec.gov*, the NASD home page at *http://www.nasd.com*, and the Federal Reserve Board website at *http://www.federalreserve.gov*.

Key Point

Automatically generated contingent orders are appealing for many reasons; but they may contradict the swing trading strategy as well.

Order Types for Swing Trading

market order
an order to buy or sell as quickly as possible and at the best available price. Execution is guaranteed, but price is not.

limit order
a type of order specifying execution of a buy at or below a specified price, or of a sell order at or above a specified price.

The *market order* is the most common order placed. With this order, you ask your broker to complete a buy or sell transaction as soon as possible and at the best available price. With a market order, you are guaranteed that the order will be executed, but the price depends on prevailing conditions, and on how quickly a stock's price is trading. For swing traders, market orders are appropriate when you want to get a position traded as soon as possible. When the setup is complete to make your swing trade, for example, the market order is the fastest way to complete it.

If you want a specific price rather than mere guarantee of execution, you may also place a *limit order*. With this order, you get your price or better. For example, if you are buying, a limit order would get you a specified price or lower; and if you are selling, a limit order would get you a specified price or higher. You can also place time restrictions on the limit order, such as requiring the order be completed within one day or not at all. Opposite the market

> ### Key Point
>
> Limit orders are appealing because they lead to execution only if and when a specified price is met or passed. While swing traders do not always apply such price-based rules, limit orders provide an alternative.

order, a limit order's price *or better* is assured, but execution is not, since your requirement might not be met. For swing trading, a limit order is a useful tool. Some setup features require movement in the stock. For example, if the price has been falling and today appears to be a narrow range day, the buy signal would take place if and when the price ticks upward. So a limit order can be useful to automatically get your position opened as early as possible in the reversal.

A popular form of time restriction to an order is the *day order*. This type specifies that if the order's conditions are not met by the end of the trading day, it expires without completion. For swing trading, this type of order can be used to limit losses or to augment potential profits when you plan to cut short the trade. If you have made a good profit, for example, and you are concerned that the price trend will reverse suddenly, you can place a day order with price limits to close out a position if and when conditions are met within the day's trend.

Another variation of the day order requires immediate action or, failing that, it will expire. The *fill or kill (FOK)* order is a term attached to a limit order telling your broker that the entire order must be executed right away or, if that is not possible, it is to be canceled. The instruction *immediate or cancel* allows the brokerage firm to fill part of your order under the same conditions. For swing trading, these are valuable tools to close out positions at the end of a two- to five-day trend *if* the end does end;

or better

in a limit order, the terms for completion of a transaction. In a buy order, execution is to occur when a specified price or lower has been reached; and with a sell order, execution is to occur when a specified price or higher has been reached.

day order

a type of order placed with a broker specifying that if it is not executed by the end of the trading day, it automatically expires.

fill or kill (FOK)

a condition attached to a limit order instructing your broker to complete the order immediately or, if that is not possible, to cancel the order right away.

immediate or cancel

a condition allowing a broker to fill part of an order if the entire order cannot be completed; and on the stipulation that this be done right away and any remaining portions canceled.

stop orders

types of orders that generate execution once a stop price has been met or passed (below for buy orders and above for sell orders). Once the stop price has been met or passed, the trade is executed.

do not reduce (DNR)

instructions attached to an order to keep a limit price even when cash dividends occur. Without the DNR, the limit price is automatically reduced for dividends earned.

or to continue riding profits if the timing is not right for the trend to stop. Some trends go beyond the indicated time window, so the fill or kill can be used in swing trading to maximize potential profits.

In the last chapter, the trailing stop and buy stop were described in the context of how swing traders can take profits if and when a trend reverses. Both of these types of *stop orders*, which are market orders with a conditional requirement: the stock must trade at or below a specified price (for buy orders) or at or above (for sell orders). This stop price is predetermined, but there is no assurance that execution will occur under those conditions. The stop generates the trade, even though the price may continue to move or reverse directions after the generating event has occurred.

Other kinds of instructions can also be attached to orders. For example, *do not reduce (DNR)* tells your broker to execute your trade at the specified limit price, and to not reduce that price when *ex-dividend* date occurs. Without a DNR, the limit price is automatically taken down to match the effect of a declared dividend.

Time limits can be placed on orders, although some brokerage firms limit how long an unfilled order can be left open. A *good 'til canceled (GTC)* instruction means just that: the order is to remain open until it can be executed on the terms you specify. Most brokerage firms will set a limit, after which GTC orders will expire.

The many special conditions, limits and contingencies attached to buy and sell orders may become an important aspect of a swing trading strategy. In picking an online brokerage service, the flexibility and range of conditional orders offered may be used as one of several criteria for selecting one company over another.

Key Point

A stop order is useful for assuring that paper profits are not lost, or for limiting exposure to risk.

Key Point

You can coordinate contingency ordering as part of a swing trading strategy, but don't allow the orders to offset the advantages of the setup and execution pattern.

Coordinating Orders with Swing Trading Strategies

Under the guidelines for swing trading, you seek a trend's setup and, when it appears, you go into action. So the combination of events creates the decision. These events include three trend days; a narrow range day or an engulfing line; and higher than average volume. However, when you use special orders, you modify the swing trading strategy. Instead of acting when the setup occurs, you program in a specific trade based on a trigger event.

This works on both sides of the transaction. You can place a *contingent order* to open a transaction as well as one to close. For example, you may

ex-dividend
the date of ownership for the purpose of paying dividends. The owner of shares on the specified date is entitled to the dividend, even if shares are sold after that date but before dividend payment date (when shares are said to be trading ex-dividend). The ex-date is the dividing point.

Key Point

Use the setup of the swing trade as your *primary* tool for identifying a decision point. The contingent order should be the exception rather than the rule.

good 'til canceled (GTC)

a condition attached to an order to leave it open indefinitely until it can be filled on the terms the investor requires; brokerage firms will let such orders expire after a specified time period.

contingent order

any order to buy or sell based on specific price levels being reached or passed. This type of order is used to protect existing profits or to avoid large losses in the event of sudden price movement.

long position

ownership of stock and other securities, entered by execution or trades in the sequence buy-hold-sell.

decide you want to enter a swing trade on a stock with a *long position*, but only if and when the stock's price falls to a specific price or below. You may also enter a *short position* in the same way, short selling the stock if and when the price meets or exceeds a predetermined level.

On the sell side, the contingent order can also be used to modify your swing trading strategy. This is a more popular use of contingent orders; you are more likely to place a stop limit order, for example, to protect *paper profits* or to avoid the risk of large losses.

Before modifying your swing trading strategy, you need to decide how much use to make of this alternative trading method. Swing trading, by definition, is a "hands-on" strategy requiring daily monitoring of stock charts and price trends. In fact, swing traders tend to be trading enthusiasts who want to spend time each day tracking stock prices and moving money in and out of positions. For this type of person, programmed trading and contingent order strategies are not appealing. Even the concept of using such orders to protect existing profits may not be an obvious choice.

A proposed modification of swing trading strategies protects your position and reduces risk while continuing to allow you to monitor prices and make decisions directly. Some guidelines:

1. *Use contingent orders for only two reasons: protect profits and avoid large losses.* The most appropriate use of contingent orders within a swing trading strategy is to take profits *if and when* price moves suddenly, or to minimize your losses. So long positions may develop paper profits, presenting swing traders with a dilemma: Do you sell now and take your profits or, if the setup has not developed, do you continue to hold the position until the

---

Key Point

One of the most attractive features of swing trading is the direct control and timing of decisions. The contingent order is a useful device, but most swing traders will prefer to time their decisions on chart patterns.

---

trend has run its course? The trailing stop is a valuable tool to protect profits if and when the stock's price begins to fall without the swing trading signal in place. Short positions become profitable when the stock price falls; but the risk is that the price may rise. In this situation, contingent orders place a ceiling on potential losses, in the event that the swing trade setup fails and you do not close the position in time to avoid a loss.

short position
the sale of stock and other securities that is eventually closed with a purchase transaction. In a short position, the sequence of events is sell-hold-buy.

2. *Do not place contingent orders that might contradict the basic swing trading strategy.* One big problem in overusing contingent orders is that they may contradict the basic swing trading ideal. Trading with contingent orders is not always the same as swing trading. Contingent orders may, in fact, prevent you from maximizing profits within the swing trade. You may want to depend on setup patterns and signals rather than on the use of contingent orders; or

paper profits
the profits in existing stock positions, which become realized profits only if and when those positions are closed.

Key Point

Contingent orders are great for protecting paper profits or preventing large losses. Beyond that, they contradict your reasons for using swing trading to time your decisions.

> ### Key Point
>
> Remember, a contingent order could be detrimental to an effective swing trading strategy, if not properly controlled.

> ### Key Point
>
> At times, the normal cyclical swings give way to momentum trading. This is where swing traders can ride profits for an extended period of time. But this could be prevented by unwise use of contingent orders.

you may be more cautious and take profits as they develop. The decision should be based on how much risk you are willing to take.

3. *Recognize both the advantages and limitations to contingent orders.* All strategies involve risk, and all protective measures—including contingent orders—provide benefits as well as problems. The benefits appear when contingent orders are used strictly to protect existing paper profits or to avoid losses in exposed short positions. The primary disadvantage is that these orders may be executed even when the swing trade patters are not complete. The two- to five-day window is only a guideline; in fact, some trends can continue far longer. At those times, swing traders may profit from riding the momentum, and recognize that the swing trade predictability is suspended for the moment. But using contingent orders, you may lose the opportunity to earn more profits by leaving transactions too soon.

risk tolerance
the level of risk an individual is able and willing to assume. Risk and potential profit are directly related and cannot be accepted, so those seeking better than average profits also need to expand their risk tolerance.

4. *Base your use of specialized orders on your own risk tolerance.* The concept of *risk tolerance* is always supposed to be a first test of any strategy. There is no justification for swing trading if the risks are

---

Key Point
No strategy works unless it is a good match for your personal risk tolerance. This includes swing trading. Some types of swing trade activity (like going short, for example) may be too risky, unless contingent orders are used as well.

too great—and do not depend on contingent orders to reduce or eliminate that risk. The risks are real and have to be accepted as part of the specific strategy.

Brokerage Rules for Swing Trading

Every brokerage firm offers its clients a variety of ways to trade. Swing traders may limit their activities to their cash assets or use *margin* to expand their trading activity. Margin trading involves borrowing money from your brokerage firm to invest, using stock as collateral for the loan. This is a form of *leverage*, which also means that using margin involves much higher risks than simply limiting your activity to available cash.

Before you will be allowed to open a margin account, you will also be required to set up the *minimum margin*. This requirement is spelled out in NASD Rule 2520 and in the New York Stock Exchange Rule 431. You are required to deposit at least $2,000 or 100 percent of the purchase price (whichever is less) in your brokerage account. Some traders—whose activity is higher than average—are required to deposit far more. (This is explained later in this chapter.)

The advantage of investing in a margin account is that it exposes you to much greater profit

margin
investing using funds borrowed from a brokerage firm, with securities in an account used as collateral.

leverage
an investing strategy using borrowed funds to broaden a portfolio beyond available cash resources.

opportunities. However, if a portfolio loses, you still have to repay the borrowed funds. If it takes longer than you expected to generate profits, you also have to pay the brokerage firm interest on the money borrowed.

Key Point

Margin trading provides investors with flexibility ... and with risk. The more you borrow, the greater the risk of loss and the greater your interest expense.

---

minimum margin

the deposit requirement to set up a margin account, which is the lesser of $2,000 or 100 percent of the security's purchase price.

Before deciding to swing trade on margin, recognize four specific risks:

1. You can suffer losses beyond the level of your cash investment.

2. You can be required to deposit additional funds into your account to cover market losses, potentially with little advance notice.

3. You could need to sell some stocks to cover falling prices in a margin account.

4. Your brokerage firm has the right to sell stock from your portfolio to repay itself, without notifying you of the decision *or* which stocks they will sell.

To open a margin account and trade on margin, your brokerage firm will require you to sign a margin agreement in advance. *Read the document* in full. Also become familiar with the margin regulations of the Securities and Exchange Commission (SEC), the National Association of Securities Dealers (NASD), and the Federal Reserve Board. The Fed governs and limits margin activity through its *initial margin* rule. This is a

---

Key Point

If you don't keep your margin account at the required level—including loss of market value in your portfolio—your brokerage firm can sell your stocks to repay itself. This can occur without advance notice, and without your decision about which stocks to sell.

---

limit of 50 percent that you can borrow on margin, and the complete terms of the Fed's margin rules are found in *Regulation T*.

You are required to maintain a specific amount of cash and equity in your account when using margin to invest. This is equal to the current market value of your securities minus the amount you owe on margin. You can never maintain an account below 25 percent of current market value of securities, a level known as *maintenance requirement* under margin rules. Some brokerage firms impose maintenance above 25 percent, often as high as 40 percent or more depending on the kinds of stocks in your portfolio. The specific amount required by your brokerage firm is called the *house requirement*.

The maintenance requirement imposed by your brokerage firm can make a big difference in the amount of cash you need in your account. For example, if you buy $16,000 in securities with $8,000 cash and $8,000 on margin, you are required to keep a maintenance level of no less than 25 percent. So if the value of your stock falls to $12,000, your equity would fall to $4,000 ($12,000 minus $8,000 loss). At a maintenance requirement of 25 percent, you are required to have at least $3,000 in equity (25 percent of $12,000). Because your equity is $4,000, your maintenance requirement is met. However, if your firm required you to maintain 40 percent, your equity would not be sufficient. You would need 40 percent of the $12,000 current market value, or $4,800. The firm would issue a *margin call* demanding that you deposit an additional $800.

A brokerage firm may also increase its maintenance requirement at any time and without advance notice. So if the firm believes that it is overly exposed to the risk of margin loss, you could be required to deposit additional funds to meet the new rules. Of course, all of the margin activity involves the payment

initial margin
a limit on the level of borrowing investors are allowed by the Federal Reserve Board's Regulation T. It specifies that you can only borrow up to 50 percent of a security's purchase price.

Regulation T
a Federal Reserve Board rule establishing and governing rules for margin borrowing in brokerage accounts.

maintenance requirement
the percentage of current market value of securities that must be kept in a portfolio at all times. Minimum federal requirement is 25 percent, but some brokerage firms require higher maintenance levels.

Key Point

Be sure you know how much cash you have to keep on deposit based on maintenance levels. This may vary from one brokerage firm to another, so you need to check in advance.

---

house requirement

the maintenance requirement set by brokerage firms, which is equal to or greater than the minimum 25 percent required under NASD and NYSE rules.

margin call

a demand from a brokerage firm for additional deposits by investors whose maintenance requirement has not been met due to portfolio losses. If the margin call is not met, the brokerage firm will sell securities from the account.

of interest to the brokerage firm, so the longer it takes for you to generate profits, the higher the cost. Most firms base their margin interest rate on the *broker call rate* published in the *Wall Street Journal* under the Money Rates section. Brokerage firms also publish their current margin rates on their websites.

Margin rules are going to vary by brokerage firm. If you plan to execute swing trades using a margin account, be aware of your firm's specific rules and requirements, and also determine whether or not you will be considered a pattern day trader (see the next section), for which requirements will be even stricter.

To check online brokerage rules for margin trading and other rules, check brokerage firm websites:

Accutrade	www.accutrade.com
American Express	www.americanexpress.com/direct
Bank One OneInvest	www.oneinvest.com
BrownCo	www.brownco.com
Charles Schwab	www.schwab.com
Cititrade	www.cititrade.com
E-Trade Financial	www.etrade.com
Fidelity	www.fidelity.com
Firstrade	www.firstrade.com
Harrisdirect	www.harrisdirect.com

Scottrade   www.scottrade.com

T. Rowe Price   www.troweprice.com

TD Ameritrade   www.tdameritrade.com

TD Waterhouse   www.tdwaterhouse.com

Vanguard   www.vanguard.com

WallStreet*E Inc.   www.wallstreete.com

broker call rate
the rate many brokers charge clients for borrowing funds on margin; the rate a firm charges is normally found on the brokerage website.

Pattern Day Trader Rules

In February 2001, the Securities and Exchange Commission (SEC) approved a new rule proposed by the New York Stock Exchange and National Association of Securities Dealers. Under Regulation T margin requirements, all calculations are performed only at the end of a trading day. Thus, a day trader can execute a high volume of trades within a trading cycle using the margin account, and avoid the margin restrictions of Regulation T. So in the event that large losses are suffered by a day trader, it is possible that brokerage firms end up absorbing those losses.

The pattern day trader is anyone who buys or sells a single security within the same trading day (a day trade) four or more times in any consecutive five trading periods. In addition, to qualify as a pattern day trader, the high-volume activity has to make up 6 percent or more of total trades. (If, for example, you have a large volume of trades but less than 6 percent of the total meets the four-or-more rule, you won't be classified as a pattern day trader.)

This rule, also known as NASD Rule 2520, comes with a very high margin requirement. Pattern day traders have to deposit and keep minimum equity of $25,000 in their accounts; and these funds must be

---

Key Point

The pattern day trader rule was established to solve the problem created when day traders opened and closed transactions in a single day. Margin requirements are computed only at the trading day's conclusion.

deposited before the high volume trading can go forward. If an investor does not meet this deposit rule, the brokerage firm can impose trading restrictions. For example, your firm can restrict your trading for 90 days to a cash-only basis, thus suspending all margin trading.

day trade call

a requirement that investors deposit funds to satisfy pattern day trading deposit requirements based on the volume of trades (four or more trades in the same security within five trading days).

If your account violates the pattern day trading requirement, you have five days to satisfy the margin call. This provision, also called the *day trade call*, may also be subject to a holding period before it can be used for subsequent trading.

Swing trading is an ideal device for avoiding the restrictive pattern day trading rule, assuming that you adhere to the normal timing curve. Setup for transactions normally involves at least three trading days to develop. The swing trading uptrend (made up of three or more days of higher closings and with a series of higher highs offset by higher lows) or downtrend (three consecutive days of lower closings and a series of lower lows offset by lower highs) are the opening side of a swing trade. But because the usual closing setup also requires three or more periods in most cases, you have a programmed six-day minimum for a complete buy-and-sell or sell-and-buy transaction.

Because pattern day trading is defined as involving the same security, in theory a swing trader will never be classified as a pattern day trader. Of course, if you do execute trades more often than the typical swing trade pattern dictates, it is easy to fall into a pattern where you would be classified under this rule. If you have $25,000 in cash and equity in your account, this is not a problem. But if your portfolio value is lower than $25,000, you need to avoid falling into this definition. Lacking funds to continue high-volume trading, your activity—including swing trades—would be restricted by your brokerage firm.

Key Point

Day trading, with its two- to five-day window, is the perfect strategy for avoiding the pattern day trading rule. By definition, the completion of a trade on both sides requires at least six trading days.

Key Point

A day trade includes not only trades during the hours the market is open, but also premarket and post-market transactions on the same day.

Under the rule, a "day trade" is defined as a buy and sell of the same security on the same day. This includes pre-market trading, transactions during market hours, *and* aftermarket trades. If you open a position today and close it tomorrow, that is not a day trade and activity in this pattern can be executed without risking being classified as a pattern day trader. The scope of the rule includes all U.S. brokers who are also members of the NASD, and covers both stock and option trades. No pattern day trading rules apply to futures trading. The rule is especially applicable to options traders who may execute a large volume of trades within a single day on the same security.

While many investors consider being classified as a pattern day trader as a penalty, there is a positive side as well. The day trade *buying power* is calculated by the brokerage firm as a multiple of an account's equity, and this may be greater than the allowance for the typical non-pattern day trader's account. For example, some brokers allow up to four times a day's closing equity. So if your equity in a trading account is $25,000 and you are a pattern day trader, your buying power would be $100,000 (assuming your broker applies the four-times formula).

buying power
the margin allowance a brokerage firm provides to a pattern day trader, which is a multiple of available equity balance in the portfolio.

The pattern day trading rule was designed to prevent investors from avoiding margin requirements based on Regulation T. Before the rule went into effect, buying power for day traders was virtually unlimited. As long as margin-based transactions were closed by the end of the day, no margin calls were generated. So day traders were able to use extreme leverage to control large positions in securities. The risk was shifted to brokerage firms because if prices moved suddenly (as they have done in single days periodically in the past) there was no way for brokerage firms to enforce margin calls. With $25,000 on deposit, the brokerage firms

> ### Key Point
>
> Check the rules imposed by brokerage firms for pattern day trading and margin requirements. If you expect to execute a large volume of transactions, this could be an important decision point.

have some security and many would-be day traders with little or no real equity were eliminated from this kind of trading activity.

Knowing how the trading rules work is useful in picking a broker and in identifying levels of risk. However, swing traders also need to determine how they will select stocks for swing trading use. This applies whether you apply the traditional long position (buying stock and holding it, to eventually close the position through a sale) or a riskier short position (selling stock, holding it, and then closing the position with a purchase). The next chapter provides suggestions for picking stocks appropriate for your swing trading strategy.

Picking Stocks
for Swing Trading

Investors and traders face a problem in deciding what stocks or indexes on which to swing trade. So how do you decide on one stock over another? With thousands of stocks to choose from, you need to identify the selection attributes to help pick a set of stocks to use. This set needs to be finite, and the actual number of stocks should depend on several factors, including:

1. *Available capital for trading.* Any program is going to be limited by the capital available to trade. Your trading capital may be separate from a long-term portfolio. Some investors put aside a small portion of available capital for short-term trading, while the majority is left to accumulate in long-term investment stocks, mutual funds, real estate and the money market.

2. *Risk tolerance level in effect.* Your personal risk tolerance level also restricts and defines the kinds of stocks you will use for swing trading. Companies with decades of experience, billions in capital, and domination in their field are relatively safe investments—yet may not be appropriate for swing trading. Relatively young companies are more likely to produce the kinds of price volatility desirable for swing trading. They can, however, be excessively risky. Most people will define their risk tolerance in such a way that their stock selections will fall in between these extremes.

Key Point

Any trading strategy—including swing trading—is limited by the capital you have available to trade. This means it is also necessary to figure out a way to limit the number of stocks you will use for trading.

Key Point

Picking appropriate stocks is a function of defining your risk tolerance level. Once you decide how much risk is appropriate, the list of potential stocks is naturally reduced as well.

---

3. *Degree of price swing and current trend.* Swing trading works in a middle zone of price volatility. If a stock's trading range is narrow and not at all volatile, swing trading opportunities will be limited. If a stock is on the other end of the spectrum—with wildly swinging prices and no established trading range, you face a different problem: The price may not conform to the usual "rules" of swing trading setup, candlestick chart formations, and other technical tools for predicting price movement. Highly volatile stocks do not always conform, so the predictability simply is not there.

4. *Personal preferences.* Everyone has their favorite stocks. You may decide to swing trade in stocks you own, or in stocks you have tracked over a period of time. You may also decide to specialize in a limited number of industries, and move between sectors based on cyclical patterns. It is important to recognize the limiting

---

Key Point

Stocks whose price is so volatile that no trading range can be easily established, are too high risk for most people—and also less viable for swing trading.

Key Point

Personal preference is part of your selection process along with other price and financially based criteria.

Key Point

Fundamental and technical analysis help you not only to pick stocks matching your risk profile, but also to eliminate companies that do not represent a good fit.

factors in following personal preferences rather than technical signals. You might tend to ignore important signals because you prefer a stock or, equally problematical, ignore a broad range of possible stocks because your personal preferences are limited.

5. *Technical and fundamental tests.* Finally, you select either fundamental or technical tests to (1) select or (2) eliminate stocks from the list of swing trading candidates. Using only one selection criterion is a mistake; you can combine numerous fundamental and technical tests to narrow your list, identify appropriate risk levels and stocks fitting those levels, and coordinate price-related trends with sound fundamental principles.

Rules of Thumb for Stock Selection

To pick stocks for swing trading, it makes sense to start by finding a range of potential companies meeting fundamental criteria. Even traders focused on the purely technical indicators of price and volume will recognize the fundamentals as an important test of (1) stock price risk, (2) capital strength or weakness, and (3) long-term price growth potential. The fundamentals are backward-looking in the sense that actual financial reporting is historical; but fundamental trends and tests of capital strength also reveal a lot about future potential on a technical level.

Key Point

It is inherently impossible to judge a company based on fundamental principles if the company has never reported a profit. The lack of success in the market may be even more profound, however; why would you buy stock in a company that has lost money every year?

Some very basic questions you will want to ask about companies before including them in a list of swing trade possibilities include issues beyond the details of revenue and earnings or current capitalization. Ask these questions as a method for narrowing your swing trading list:

1. *Has the company ever reported a net profit?* At a minimum requirement, a listed company should report profitable operations. Some corporations have loss years, and that may be part of a normal cycle in operations. Some companies have *never* reported a profit. This means that current value is all based on potential for future growth, and this is where a lot of trouble may come into the price equation. The dot.com years make this lesson well; a company should have reported profits at some point in the recent past before it should be seriously considered for swing trading.

2. *Has corporate management been scandal-free?* Recent history has shown that many prestigious corporations may be led poorly. It makes no sense to trade in the stock of a company with questionable accounting or whose management is under investigation. Such problems distort price and may also distort the normal cyclical trends, making it impossible to time and predict how price is going to behave in the short term.

Key Point

Corporate scandals are not only in the past. Any evasiveness or questionable activity should be a red flag for anyone thinking about investing in a company.

> ## Key Point
>
> A well-managed company should be able to manage its rate of growth; this means that revenue and earnings should be consistent and not highly volatile from year to year.

3. *Have earnings been fairly consistent, or irregular?* A sound test of a company's stability is consistency. Have revenues and earnings been steady and regular? Or are annual results erratic and inconsistent? A lot of emphasis is placed on price volatility but *fundamental volatility* is also an important test. Erratic reported earnings are a sign of poor management, questionable accounting change, or turmoil within the company. Any of these may affect the dependability of price trends as well.

fundamental volatility
the degree of consistency or change in reported revenues and earnings from one year to the next.

Also check *core earnings* to determine a corporation's reporting consistency. These earnings, calculated by Standard & Poor's, are reported as part of the S&P stock report summaries offered free of charge on some discount brokerage websites, such as Charles Schwab & Company (*http://www.schwab.com*). The consistency in core earnings is equally as important as fully-reported earnings.

core earnings
the earnings as reported by a company, adjusted to remove all reported earnings that are not part of a corporation's "core" business, including nonrecurring revenues and net earnings.

4. *Is the company a leader in its industry? Does it offer a product that is not becoming obsolete?* Competition often defines profitability. So a corporation that leads its industry has many attributes that manifest in the stock price. As the industry leader's price rises or falls, the rest of the competitors in the same industry tend to follow suit. A company does not have to be number one in the industry to justify swing trading; but the leader often sets the tone of trading for many other companies.

Key Point
It makes sense to concentrate on sector leaders for swing trading. There is a tendency for nonleaders in the sector to follow and track the leading company's stock.

Over time, some products suffer from obsolescence. This is unavoidable. However, if a company is not able to change with the times, its entire product line is at risk. For example, a few years ago Polaroid filed bankruptcy. It had created a revolution with the instant photo industry but did not keep pace with the emerging digital technology. And Kodak, historically dominant in the film sales business, has in recent years also fallen behind as many competitors have passed the company in development of digital technology—meaning that to some degree, Kodak was so dependent on its film lines that it failed to recognize how significantly the whole business was changing. These types of emerging changes in technology provide a glimpse of how corporations evolve over time or, in some cases, fall behind their more aggressive competitors. This affects value in the long time as well as price trends in the short term. Even though swing trading is a short-term trading strategy, it makes sense to limit this activity to corporations that are competitive and well managed, and that are most likely to have stock price behavior in line with "typical" or "average" short-term trends.

5. *Is the company diversified? Is it vulnerable to cyclical problems?* There are many forms of *diversification*. Most people think about placing capital in several different products as the most obvious form of diversification. But this may also refer to investing in dissimilar markets or products; avoiding stocks vulnerable to the same cycles; or allocating money to entirely different markets. Within the corporation itself, diversification refers to dissimilar product or service lines of business. For example, Altria Corporation (MO) is best-known for its Phillip Morris line of business, but it also owns Kraft Foods, which diversifies its overall holdings into an entirely dissimilar market. So, in terms of how you pick stocks, the question of *internal diversification* is as important as the portfolio-related forms most investors understand well.

Key Point

Diversification comes in many forms. From the corporate perspective, diversification by product lines is a good way to offset cyclical change and to expand outside of a primary industry.

A company not well diversified is vulnerable to cyclical changes. For example, a retail corporation is going to suffer when consumer buying trends are in a down cycle, so one way to offset this cyclical problem is through diversification into lines other than the primary retail line.

6. *What current problems does the company face?* Other than the current and historical financial reports, what else do you need to know when picking companies? Is there any ongoing legal problem or potential labor union disputes? Companies dependent on large unionized labor forces are vulnerable to strikes, for example. And extensive litigation also adversely affects profitability. Merck (MRK) had thousands of outstanding lawsuits as of 2006 due to the widely advertised ill effects of its drug Vioxx. And the tobacco industry has faced thousands of lawsuits over many years. These issues may adversely affect a company's value or, if the company prevails or suffers less than expected in judgments of these lawsuits, stock prices could also rise. So the existence of thousands of lawsuits is not, by itself, reason to avoid a company or an industry. However, it is one of the extra-financial factors to be considered. Besides lawsuits, any other form of *contingent liability* may affect value and perceived value of a company, and should be reviewed as part of your judgment to buy or not.

diversification
one of several methods of spreading risk, involving exposure to different products, markets, or stocks. For corporations, diversification also refers to investment in dissimilar lines of business.

internal diversification
a form of corporate diversification of capital into dissimilar product or service lines of business.

contingent liability
a liability that might or might not materialize, and whose dollar value may not be known. Typically, outstanding lawsuits that have not been settled or decided are the best-known form of such contingencies.

Key Point
Look beyond the numbers. Read the footnotes in the annual report and track financial news to discover any special circumstances that could affect a company's stock price.

Key Point
There is much to be said for a track record. For swing trading, the ability to view a company's price history may be an important determining factor in picking one stock over another.

7. *Has the company been in business long enough to have a track record?* In selecting one stock over another, it is impossible to make a sound judgment without a track record. How long has the company been in business? Can you tell whether there has been growth in net worth, or a reduction? What is the reputation of management? Does the company pay dividends, and what is the current dividend yield? Have dividend payments been consistent, or have some been missed? These questions define corporations and provide you with a means for comparison and selection.

Fundamental and Technical Indicators

A combination of some basic fundamental and technical indicators can be useful in narrowing down the list of swing trading stocks. If your selection criteria are too broad, there will be too many stocks to choose from. Ideally, a group of between 10 and 25 stocks meeting all of your criteria is a fair range, especially if they represent a diversified cross-section of market sectors.

If you are able to check a stock's fundamental strength using only four or five indicators, it is a sound number. Too many indicators can make it difficult to pick stocks, if only because you will have to spend too much time running and monitoring your tests. Suggested fundamental indicators include:

> ### Key Point
>
> Limit the number of indicators you use for picking stocks. If you pick too many, your analytical task will be more daunting and exclusionary.

1. *Revenue and earnings.* A sound, basic starting point is revenue and earnings, or the top and bottom lines of the *operating statement*. This is a *financial statement* summarizing of all activity for a specific period of time (year, quarter, or month). If you check revenue and earnings over a period of time, you can identify whether a company is growing consistently; reporting erratic results; or flatlining in its results.

operating statement

a financial statement summarizing all activity—revenue, costs and expenses, and profits—for a specified period of time, most often a full year or a fiscal quarter.

For example, revenue and earnings for Lucent Technologies (LU) was erratic for the five years between 2001 and 2005, as shown in Figure 6.1.

financial statement

a report published by a corporation reporting activity over a period of time, such as a full year (the operating statement) or balances of asset, liability and net worth accounts at the end of a period (the balance sheet).

Note the wide swings from year to year in both revenue and earnings. Lucent's five-year history has been quite volatile, not only with drastic reductions in reported revenue, but also with large changes in net losses and profits.

In comparison, Wal-Mart (WMT) has reported revenue and earnings with remarkable consistency, as shown in Figure 6.2. In this example, both revenue and earnings have increased steadily over a period of years, making Wal-Mart's financial results far more predictable than Lucent's.

2. *Dividend yield.* The overall profit you earn from, buying stocks is not limited to the *capital gains* from buying and selling shares of stock. If you hold stock for any length of time, you also need to compare *dividend yield* on the stock. This form of profit, also called *current yield*, can represent a major portion of overall yield.

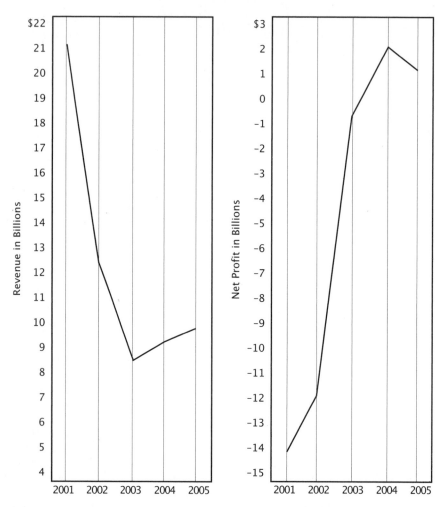

FIGURE 6.1 Erratic Revenue and Earnings: Lucent Technologies
Source: Standard & Poor's Stock Reports.

The dividend is normally paid quarterly to stockholders of record on the declaration date. A dividend may vary from zero up to a significant percentage. One method for selecting stocks is to seek higher than average yields. This is one method for finding companies with healthy *cash flow* and profits. A corporation cannot pay out dividends unless it has funds available; so high-yielding dividends among companies that meet other fundamental tests is an effective method for narrowing down your list.

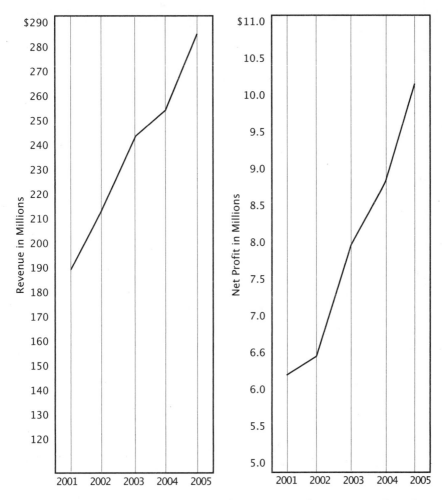

FIGURE 6.2 Consistent Revenue and Earnings: Wal-Mart Stores (WMT)
Source: Standard & Poor's Stock Reports.

Valuable Resource

To find high-yielding stocks to invest in for periods longer than the usual swing-trading term, check Mergent Corporation's Dividend Achiever's publications at *http://www.dividendachievers.com* or Dogs of the Dow at *http://www.dogsofthedow.com*.

dividend yield

the profit earned from dividends paid by corporations, expressed as a percentage of the current price. For calculation purposes, the percentage should always be based on stock purchase price rather than current price.

current yield

the percentage paid in dividends, calculating by dividing declared dividends by current price of the stock.

cash flow

the cash available from operations to pay current and long-term expenses and liabilities; fund business expansion; and pay dividends.

3. *P/E ratio.* The price-to-earnings ratio, or the *P/E ratio*, is a popular test of a company's current price. It is a comparison of a technical factor (the current stock price) to a fundamental factor (earnings per share). The *multiple* (the result of dividing price by earnings) is an expression of the market's expectation for future growth. That is, the higher the multiple, the greater the long-term risk. One selection method for stocks is to limit the range of the P/E multiple. For example, you may decide to limit your stocks for swing trading to those with multiples between 11 and 25.

4. *Debt ratio.* One of the most critical tests of corporate health is a study of the trend involving types of *capitalization.* A company may fund its operations through equity capital (selling stock) or debt capital (issuing bonds or taking out long-term loans). All debt capital has to be repaid with interest, so the higher the percentage of debt, the greater the strain on future cash. If debt capital is too high, future expansion will be hampered, and as more profits have to be paid in interest there will be less remaining for dividends. So the *debt ratio* is one of the most important fundamental tests you can perform. To compute, divide the balance of *long-term liabilities* by total capitalization (long-term

Key Point

The P/E ratio should be viewed over a period of years and quarters to establish a trend. It compares *current* price to the *latest* reported earnings, so its interim reliability is questionable. Use yearend P/E to identify the actual trend and relationship between price and earnings.

debts plus shareholders' equity), expressing the result as a percentage. If this percentage is rising over time, that is a negative sign.

Limiting the fundamentals is important because, with too much information, you cannot make important distinctions between companies. A few solid, important tests that cover the questions of profitability and capital strength are adequate to pick stocks. The same argument applies to technical indicators. In this realm, your goal is quite different, however. With the fundamentals, you seek signs of strength and consistent profits. On the technical side, you want stocks that are not wildly volatile, but are also not flat. The selection of worthwhile technical indicators includes:

P/E ratio

a test comparing technical and fundamental information. The price per share is divided by earnings per share to arrive at the multiple. The P/E is an effective way to compare stocks and to limit stock selection. The result of dividing price per share by earnings per share is expressed as a single numerical value, known as the multiple.

1. *Trading range.* The most basic of price indicators is the trading range. A very narrow trading range, indicating low volatility, defines a stock as low risk; and a broad trading range, indicating high volatility, defines a stock as high risk. A stock that is so volatile that no specific trading range can be found is extremely high risk.

   For swing trading, you want to find stocks with moderate levels of volatility. If you equate volatility with interest in a stock, you can appreciate why moderate volatility makes sense. When both buyers and sellers are interested in the stock, a never-ending struggle to control the price is expressed through the two- to five-day cycles. Buyers want the price to move up after they buy, and sellers want to see price fall only after they sell. It is important to also recognize

multiple

the P/E of a stock, arrived at by dividing price per share by earnings per share. The multiple is expressed as a single numerical value.

capitalization

the total funding of an operation, include equity (stock) and debt (bonds and long-term loans).

that buyers become sellers, and vice versa, when price movement suits an investor's interests. If volatility is too low, this tells you there is little interest in the stock; and if volatility is too high, it is most difficult to decide the direction of the short-term price cycles.

Key Point

There is no need to exclude technical indicators just because you look to the fundamentals. The most effective analysis uses both sides to improve perspective on value, volatility and risk.

---

debt ratio

the portion of capitalization represented by debt; to compute, divide long-term liabilities by total capitalization, expressing the result as a percentage.

long-term liabilities

all liabilities due and payable beyond the next 12 months (the current portion), including notes, contracts and bonds.

2. *Direction of the channel.* A price channel is the parallel movement of the trading range. If you are going to open swing trades with long positions, you will be most interested in stocks whose channels are moving upward. If the channel is flat but trades can be made within that trading range, it does not matter whether you open positions on long or short sides; you can begin with either, or use both depending on the formation and setup patterns that emerge.

3. *Recent history of short-term swing prices.* The historical volatility provides no guarantees of future price direction. But it does provide you with some sense of how the price acts and moves—the timing of up and down movements, degree of change, and the importance of changes in daily volume along with dramatic price movement.

4. *Recent patterns, including breakouts and price gaps.* Technical patterns are interesting not only because they provide buy or sell signals, but also because they allow you to anticipate the next move with some assurance. Breakouts and price gaps are among the most important technical indicators because they often are seen at the start of a new trend. Even a minor price gap may signal a big change in direction, and price breakouts above resistance or below support are invariably significant. The stronger the breakout pattern, the stronger the trend is likely to be. When breakout is accompanied with one or more price gaps, it represents a very strong short-term change in the price level. This is when swing trading can be most profitable.

Short-Term Versus Long-Term Indicators

There is a distinction every trader needs to make. This comes from coordinating the long-term fundamental and technical indicators with short-term setup signals for swing trading. The two are so entirely different that the criteria cannot be ignored.

You begin by determining which stocks to include in the realm of swing trading possibilities. It may be that you will want to acquire and hold some of these stocks as well. This long-term determination must be limited because most people cannot afford to own thousands of stocks or even hundreds. Acquiring shares of a few stocks must suffice, so you need to identify the criteria you are going to use as a starting point.

The setup signals for swing trading can be found on hundreds of stocks, indexes and exchange traded funds. This does not mean you will want to try and make trades in a random and undisciplined manner. One dilemma for swing traders is deciding how to limit their range of activity. By first deciding how to pick stocks, you can achieve the necessary limitations. Five guidelines to keep in mind:

1. *Apply basic fundamental and technical criteria.* Earlier in this chapter, a handful of key indicators were provided with the purpose of demonstrating how you can *limit* the range of analysis in picking stocks—both for long-term investing and swing trading. You may discover that the criteria for both are the same. Even if your intention is to swing trade and not to hold any stocks in your portfolio, your risk profile should always dominate the way you pick stocks, even if you intend to move in and out of positions in the typical two- to five-day window. The criteria set limits on the range of stocks you will use for swing trading. If you end up with approximately 15 to 20 stocks that you follow regularly and monitor for swing trading opportunities—and all meet your analytical criteria—you will have your hands full. It is unlikely that you will ever face a situation where no swing trading setups occur.

Key Point

The goals you use for picking long-term investments are not the same as that for picking stocks to swing trade. The same criteria, however, may be used to pick stocks that work for both purposes.

---

2. *Make value judgments about sectors of stocks.* Every investor experiences a bias concerning groups of stocks. You might be fearful of investing in sectors such as retail, oil and gas, or computers, for example. These biases may be based on past experience or on a sense of greater than average risk. Some sectors are clearly higher risk than others in certain economic times. Whether your biases are rational or not, you should avoid sectors that:

   a. You are uncomfortable with.

   b. You believe are high risk.

   c. Whose attributes you do not understand well.

3. *Focus on sector leaders.* Within a particular sector, it makes sense to swing trade in the issues considered to be the leaders. There is a sound reason for this: The nonleading stocks in a sector tend to follow the general direction of the leading stocks. For the purposes of swing trading, it makes sense to focus on those leaders to get clear setup signals. Some swing traders focus on sector indices and funds, but this is less effective. When you trade an ETF for one sector, for example, you are trading a mix of all the stocks, both strong and weak; so the net result includes offsetting trends. It is more effective to trade in single stocks to make the most of swing trading.

4. *Distinguish between speculation and swing trading activity.* Then pure speculative play is often a coin toss. Even speculators who use various forms of analysis tend to favor undiscovered opportunities in smaller, emerging issues. Many of these companies have never reported a profit and usually do not have a track record. They may also lack a clear trading range history. For that reason, important tests such as volatility, "typical" daily volume, and institutional holdings cannot be compared and tested. Swing trading is entirely different. The tendency in price patterns is more easily recognized among well established stocks, whose trading range is easily observed, and whose holdings include both institutional and retail investors. This does not mean you shouldn't swing trade on speculative stocks. However, doing so simply involves more speculative risk, and that is an important distinction.

5. *Use appropriate trading modes.* The majority of investors think in terms of the traditional long position. The sequence of events

is buy-hold-sell. But the short position—with the sequence sell-hold-buy—is equally important in short selling. In fact, one half of all short selling opportunities occur at the top of the two-to five-day cycle, when a sell setup occurs. So one choice is to enter positions only on the long side; another is to employ strategies that also enable you to swing trade by opening positions when stocks are expected to decline in price. There are two ways to achieve this:

a. *Short selling.* First is by short selling the stock, which is a considerably higher-risk strategy than buying stock. Short selling is explained in the next chapter.

b. *Options.* The second way is by using put options. When you buy a put, you profit if and when the stock's price declines. Options can provide a valuable alternative to buying and selling shares of stock, and can vastly expand your potential profits from swing trading. Chapters 8 and 9 explain how options can be used in your swing trading program.

Price Volatility and the "Perfect" Swing Trade Stock

In seeking the right stocks for swing trading, you face two goals, which may be contradictory. You need enough volatility to create the setups you need to make those short-term moves in and out of the stock; in other words, you need to be able to trade on the emotions of other traders and to have those emotions. You also need to have some considerable market interest. At the same time, you do not want to take up positions in stocks that are higher risk than you want to assume.

Key Point

Picking the most appropriate volatility level for swing trading depends on both the trading range and degree of change. Trading range is the more important of these two.

The "perfect" swing trade stock should contain a degree of volatility adequate for those short-term price variations, but without the high volatility you see with higher-risk stocks. Compare the one-year charts for two stocks, General Motors (GM) and Coca-Cola (KO). The first, General Motors, is shown in Figure 6.3

In a one-year period, GM experienced nearly 100 percent volatility in its stock price. (This is computed by dividing the difference between high and low prices, by the low price; in GM's case, the 18 point spread is divided by 18.5, the low, for volatility of 97 percent.) This price history is considered high risk by most technicians. Note also the three long-term price channels, which during the year were all extreme in their direction. There were virtually no periods in which prices settled down. The trading range was continually about eight points wide.

In comparison, Coca-Cola's chart is far calmer. The one-year summary for the same period is shown in Figure 6.4.

The price range in this case is only about five points, between 39 and 44. Volatility is approximately 14 percent, far lower than the previous GM example. The price variation for Coca-Cola was adequate for swing trading, even though some other stocks' volatility may have been more suitable for a high-volume swing trader.

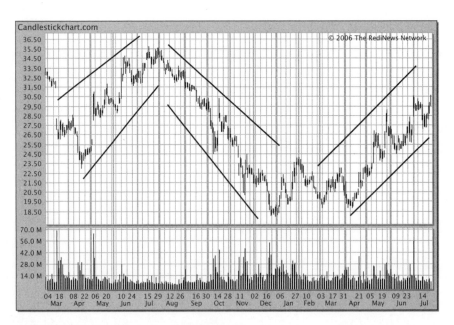

FIGURE 6.3 Volatility: General Motors

Source: Candlestickchart.com.

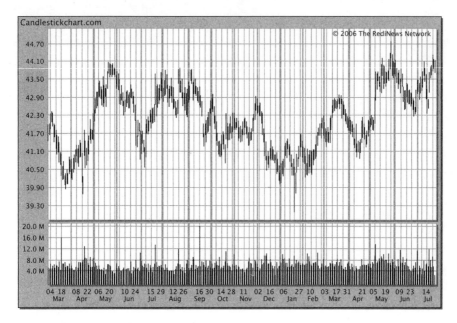

FIGURE 6.4 Calm Volatility: Coca-Cola
Source: Candlestickchart.com.

A comparison between these two stocks makes the point that volatility in price defines appropriate stocks for swing trading. While you may conclude that General Motors is higher risk than Coca-Cola, it does not always mean that swing trading is appropriate for one and not for the other. It is a matter of where your personal risk profile fits. If you are too conservative, you will not be able to find any stocks for which swing trading works; and if you seek aggressive price volatility, then you also need to accept greater market risk.

Key Point

The stocks you pick for swing trading depend largely on your perception of risk (especially when defined in degrees of volatility). What is appropriate depends on how much risk you are willing to take.

For each person entering into a swing trading strategy, the definition of the "perfect" stock should rest with a study of price volatility and trading range. For some, the five-point range for Coca-Cola would not be great enough in terms of volatility. For others, the 18-point General Motors trading range would be too high with 97 percent volatility. An analysis of many stocks will lead you to "medium-range" volatility stocks. This means averages of 20 to 40 percent volatility in a 12-month period by some definitions. Given the extreme examples of General Motors and Coca-Cola, this assumed mid-range volatility is realistic.

You will find volatility levels all over the place. A check of four stocks covering the same year as General Motors and Coca-Cola revealed the following trading ranges and volatility levels:

Altria (MO)	62–80	29%
Citigroup (C)	43–51	19%
Merck (MRK)	26–40	54%
Pfizer (PFE)	20–29	45%

Note that volatility levels and price ranges differ. An eight-point range for Citigroup in the 40s price level creates a 19 percent outcome; but virtually the same point spread, nine points for Pfizer in the 20s price range, represents a 45 percent volatility. This brings up an important point of distinction between trading range and volatility. The actual volatility cannot and should not be limited to the percentage computed on 12-month price spread. You also need to consider the point value in the trading range. The General Motors 18-point trading range was quite high compared with the Coca-Cola five-point range, for example. This would be true regardless of volatility percentages.

Key Point

The percentage of volatility is deceptive because its level depends on the price trading range. The breadth and point spread of the trading range is a more reliable risk indicator.

This observation works by making more volatile stocks appear less so as well. Altria, for example, traded between 62 and 80 but reported volatility of only 29 percent. But its price range was 18 points, the same as General Motors. In comparison, Pfizer's nine-point range produced a 45 percent volatility rate. These disparities are caused by the base price levels of each stock.

In comparing price volatility between stocks, the formula for developing volatility percentages may be useful in some regards, but it can also be misleading. It makes more sense to compare volatility between stocks in terms of the actual trading range and the extremes of price channels.

The next chapter takes the discussion into an analysis of short selling within a swing trading strategy. This is followed by two chapters explaining how you can use options to expand your strategy and bring flexibility into the program.

Selling Short

Entering a Swing Trade with a Short Order

Swing trading transactions can be entered with one of two timing beliefs: (1) the price is about to rise or (2) the price is about to fall. If you think the price will rise, you go long, meaning buying the stock. If your timing is correct, the price will rise and you can close the position at a profit. If you think the price is going to fall, then you need to *go short*, meaning opening the transaction with a sell order.

In the series of transaction possibilities, the long position involves two well-known sides. When your order is defined as *buy to open* it means the first side of the transaction is long. And this position is ended with an offsetting *sell to close* order.

On the short side, the orders occur in the opposite sequence. So the first transaction is called *sell to open*, which simply means going short on the security. This is closed with an offsetting *buy to close* order.

For many people not familiar with the concept of going short, this is a confusing idea. The question often is raised, "How can I sell something

go short
a transaction beginning with a sell order, to later close with an offsetting buy order.

buy to open
the first order in a long position, which instructs the broker to purchase the indicated security and number of shares or contracts.

> **Key Point**
>
> Short selling is simply the opposite of going long. The sequence of short selling events is: sell-hold-buy.

sell to close
an order that closes a long investment, which involves selling the security and number of shares to cancel out the open position.

sell to open
the first order in a short position, which instructs the broker to sell the indicated security and number of shares or contracts.

buy to close
an order that closes a short investment, which involves buying the security and number of shares to cancel out the open position.

I don't own?" The answer is that when you go short, it obligates you to one of several future actions. These include (1) closing the position with a buy order to cancel the short; or (2) in the case of options, accepting exercise by a buyer on the other side. (There is more on this in the next chapter.)

The Reverse Sequence

Imagine going into the real estate market and finding a house for sale; finding a buyer and entering into a contract; selling that house to the buyer; and *only then* buying the house from its current owner.

Such action is difficult to comprehend and, in fact, might even be illegal. In this example, you have no legal right to sell the property or accept money for it because you do not own it. But in the stock market, you can do just that, and as a swing trader one half of the potential transactions you will enter are going to be on the short side.

This occurs because you are trading on the uptrend *and* downtrend of a stock, and depending on the fear and greed of other investors. If you use only the buy setup, you will capitalize on only one half of your opportunities, so going short is just as important to swing trading as going long. In the next chapter, you will see why shorting the stock may not always be necessary; however, to make that decision for yourself, you need to first review how short selling works, identify the risks that are involved, and determine whether short selling is appropriate for you.

Key Point

Selling something you don't own is not allowed in most circumstances. The stock market is one exception; it is simply a matter of the *sequence* of events being different.

Here is how the procedure works. To sell a stock short, you first need to borrow the stock. So if you want to short 100 shares, your brokerage firm buys those shares in your behalf. You sell the borrowed shares on the market. If the swing trade is well timed, the stock's value will fall and you can close out the position at a profit. If your timing is off and the stock price rises, you need to either sell at a loss or wait out the timing of the price trend. This could lead to problems if your read of the chart was wrong, which will certainly happen sometimes.

For example, in Figure 7.1, a six-month chart for Walgreen Company is shown. There were numerous points in this period when the setup appeared indicating the stock was likely to fall; and yet momentum continued to carry the stock upward.

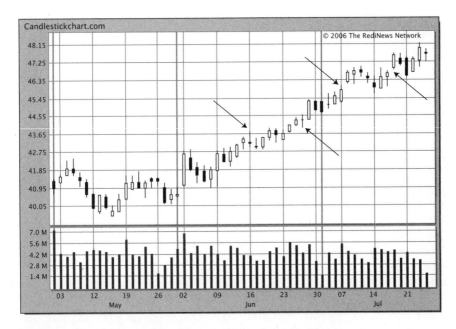

FIGURE 7.1 Setup Signals: Walgreen's Six-Month Chart

Source: Candlestickchart.com.

Key Point

Regardless of how you enter a swing trade, it ideally takes only five days at most to close up. Beyond that, it might be wise to cut losses and leave the transaction.

In this case, selling short could have resulted in a loss. From the beginning of the period to its end, the stock rose eight points. The setup signals are not always clear and you cannot expect a 100 percent success rate from swing trading. While the false signal may occur only a small portion of the time, this illustration makes the point that short selling does involve risk.

Some traders will accept the risk of short selling, recognizing that using confirmation indicators, it is possible to avoid losses most of the time, or minimize them by curtailing the activity. Remembering that swing trading is designed to complete opening and closing transaction within five days or less, it makes sense to cut losses when they do occur.

The other procedural aspect to short selling involves borrowing the stock in order to sell it. This involves a cost. Your brokerage firm charges interest based on the value of the borrowed stock, the holding period, and its current interest rate. Based on the minimal rule in effect for margin borrowing, you are required to deposit at least 50 percent of the stock's value. If the value rises, your brokerage firm will require additional sums to be left on deposit to cover this margin requirement. The outstanding borrowed stock remains subject to interest payments and margin requirements until the short position is covered, meaning shares are bought to close the position.

In addition to the margin requirement, short selling is also somewhat restricted by federal rules. The *uptick rule* was introduced as part of the Securities Exchange Act of 1934 and is known as Rule 10a-1. It states that you can only sell stock short on an uptick or a *zero-plus tick*. In other words, you can only enter a short sell if the last traded price was higher than the one preceding it. The purpose

uptick rule
a Securities and Exchange Commission (SEC) rule limiting short selling activity to prevent price manipulation; stock can be sold short only when the latest trade was higher than the trade preceding it.

of this rule was to prevent short sellers from placing downward price pressure on the stock simply by selling short, which would create greater profits with higher levels of short selling. So when you enter a short sale order, you know that the order will be filled only if and when an uptick occurs in the stock.

zero-plus tick
price movement of a stock when price rises at least in its minimum increment in the latest trade.

Risks of Short Selling

Short selling, also called "shorting" a stock, is designed to create profits when your timing is correct and the stock's price falls. Most people are more familiar with the concept of going long or buying a stock in the hope that its market value will rise. While short selling may be just as profitable as buying shares of stock, the transaction is far more complex and involves considerably greater risks than long positions.

With these risks in mind, some swing traders prefer to avoid short selling and focus only on looking for the buy setup. This is a more conservative approach than using both long and short opening positions. In either event, the margin requirement states that at least 50 percent of the stock's value must be deposited with your brokerage firm. However, risk on the short side is in theory unlimited (the stock could conceivably rise in value indefinitely) whereas long-side risk is limited. The ultimate loss would be held to the amount of money invested, assuming the stock's market value could fall to zero. A more realistic point of view, however, would curtail potential long-side risk even more, to tangible book value.

For example, a stock sells today at $55 per share. A short sale has unknown risks because that stock's price per share could rise indefinitely. The maximum long-side risk is $55 per share; but tangible book value is $20, so a realistic maximum risk is $35 per share.

Key Point

Looked at in the isolation of short selling, going short on stock is equal with going long. But in practice, risks are far higher.

Risk comparisons are difficult to make for swing trading. In theory, at least, the swing trading market risk is identical on both the uptrend and downtrend. As long as setup strength is identical on either side, you do not care whether the stock price is a reaction to fear or greed; the timing strategy remains the same. However, once you begin working within the position itself—going long or short in the stock—the risk picture changes dramatically. Short selling stock involves far greater risks than buying shares.

Short selling is not accurately viewed as being "equal" to long positions as part of a swing trading strategy, given these differences in risk levels. Short selling is often used by investors as part of a broader strategy or *hedge,* one of many strategies in which a position is taken to offset risk in a different position. For example, if you own stock and the price moves up significantly, you might sell stock short to profit from a short-term correction, but without having to sell shares you are holding long. Short selling of stock is also used to offset positions by options traders and is used for numerous reasons by hedge funds.

hedge

a position taken in a security to offset or eliminate risks in another position. For example, going short may be used as a way to protect paper profits in long positions.

The risk is each side to the strategy also has to be viewed by swing traders regarding dividend income. A short seller never receives a dividend; although that represents a potentially important portion of overall gain. In comparison, when you are in a long position, you do earn dividends as long as you own the stock on or before ex-dividend date. One variation on swing trading may involve the trading of shares with this ex-date in mind, given the adjustment made to stock price value once dividends are accounted for. For a view of risks involving short selling, however, the disadvantage that short sellers do not receive or earn dividends may be considerable.

Key Point

Short sellers do not earn dividends, a point that becomes important if you end up owning the stock for more than a few days.

The market risk for short sellers is similarly not limited to the swing trade itself. Even when you time your transactions based on setup signals on charts, outside influences often distort stock prices. For example, if a large number of short sellers *cover* their positions at the same time—meaning buying shares to close the short—this may create an artificial demand, driving up share prices and nullifying the swing trade's timing.

cover

a short seller's action in buying to close, in which the exposed short position is covered through cancellation.

The sudden cover of many short positions may be caused by normal supply and demand forces within the market for those shares; or it may be deliberately brought on by institutional investors, notably by hedge funds. For example, fund management may track what is called *short interest*—the volume of short sales in a particular stock—and may observe a rise in short positions on a particular stock and, in response, buys many shares. This drives up the share price and panic by short sellers, resulting in high volume of cover. The hedge fund then profits from the higher price of the stock. This represents a variation on market risk for swing traders in short positions. One market theory, called the "short interest theory," is based on the belief that a rapid growth in short interest foretells a rise in price.

A distinction is worth remembering regarding short selling risk. Many short sellers are merely speculating on the market and attempting to profit from a general decline in the stock's price. In comparison, swing traders would go short only if and when an appropriate setup appears. So, although these two traders have dissimilar attributes and methods for making decisions, they are subject to

short interest

a market indicator, reporting the number of shares of a specific stock that are sold short and open, and often used by investors to time market decisions.

Key Point

Swing traders act on the premise that specific setup signals lead to timing decisions. But when you sell stock short, the price could be manipulated by other investors, distorting the swing trade.

the same market forces. The actions among speculators in short positions may affect swing traders negatively, even when they respond to the clearest of setups.

Short Selling Variations

If you own shares of a stock, this makes it easier to trade on the short side. Swing trading is normally associated with fast in-and-out positions, but some swing trading also takes place among investors who also own shares.

There are often sound reasons for this. For example, if you own shares of stock that you want to hold for the long-term, you may swing trade to offset momentary price declines on the downside, *and* to take profits on the upside without needing to sell shares. Swing trading is, in fact, an appropriate and acceptable strategy when you do want to take profits but you don't want to sell the stock.

against the box
a strategy for going short when the trader owns shares. The short sale is made against the shares in the portfolio rather than borrowed from another investor.

In this situation, you can sell short *against the box*. Because you already own the shares, you don't need to borrow them in order to sell short. The term derives from the past when share certificates were issued and kept in a safe deposit box. The against the box strategy allows you to go short without (1) borrowing shares and paying interest to your brokerage firm; and (2) selling shares you'd rather keep in your portfolio.

One problem with any form of short selling is that it easily invites manipulation of stock prices. The previous example—when large investors buy shares upon observing increase in short interest—

Key Point

Swing trading is usually perceived as a strategy not including ownership of stock. But for those who do own shares, swing trading can be used to protect or to even take paper profits.

Key Point

Long investors have to look out for the "pump and dump." And short sellers have to be on guard against the short equivalent, the "short and distort."

---

may have the effect of driving prices up as short sellers panic and cover their positions. Many investors are familiar with the *pump and dump*—techniques for artificially inflating the price of a stock after buying shares in order to drive up prices—when speculators take long positions. The offsetting strategy on the short side, often called the *short and distort*—involves going short and then taking actions to scare other investors, with the intent of driving down the stock price. Anyone going short should be aware of the potential for attempted price manipulation on the part of unethical traders.

pump and dump

a strategy to buy shares and then spread rumors intended to drive up prices, after which shares are sold at a profit.

Both the SEC and NASD have drafted regulations to curtail manipulation of stock prices through pump and dump and through short and distort types of practices. But with investment chat lines widely available online, it is difficult to capture all of the abuses. Swing traders are wise to responds to setup chart signals and to ignore rumors passed around on the Internet.

The next two chapters propose an alternative to short selling, involving the use of options in place of both long and short stock positions. With options, a limited amount of capital can be used to vastly expand your swing trading portfolio, but

short and distort

a short position variation of the pump and dump strategy; speculators open short positions and then spread rumors intended to frighten investors into selling their stock to drive prices down. After the price falls, short positions are covered at a profit.

with much less risk. While options are not appropriate for everyone, their wise but limited use involves lower risks than both long and short stock positions—and they can produce the same level of profits.

Chapter

Options for Swing Trading

The Basics

Many people have only heard about the negative side of options—as high-risk, exotic instruments that are only for the most experienced speculators. This is an inaccurate description of the options market. In fact, swing traders find that using options makes perfect sense for several reasons.

An *option* is an intangible contract that grants its owner specific rights to either buy or sell stock. Every option is tied to 100 shares of a specific stock and cannot be transferred. The option's life is limited and it ceases to exist at a known date in the future. After that date, the option becomes worthless.

Swing traders face a triple dilemma in using stocks directly for swing trading:

> **option**
> an intangible contract granting its owner specific rights to either buy or sell 100 shares of a specific stock, on or before a specific date, for a specific price per share.

1. *The high risk of short selling.* First, half of all your swing trading opportunities begin as selling setups, meaning you need to go short. And short selling is a high-risk move in the market, so many swing traders limit themselves to only acting on buy setups, which cuts out half of the entire market.

Key Point

When you use stocks for swing trading, you are naturally limited in how much trading you can do, and in how much risk you can afford.

---

2. *Capital is limited.* The second problem is that with limited capital, you can only enter a small number of swing trades at any one time; this means that robust market movement cannot be fully exploited. If you buy 100 shares in any one trade, you cannot exceed your cash and margin capabilities while pursuing swing trades.

3. *You may suffer losses.* When you buy 100 shares of stock as part of a swing trade, you respond to setup signals and, if all goes well, the price rises and you sell at a profit. But there are times when the signals will not work, and you will lose money. When this happens, you have to sell and accept the loss, or hold on to those shares hoping that the price will rebound.

All of these problems and limitations can be solved using options.

A Few Definitions

Buying stock is the best-known form of *equity investment*. Each share of stock is a very small piece of ownership in a much larger whole, the corporation. A swing trader is less concerned with the long-term ramifications of equity investment, including the earning of dividends and voting rights. His or her concern is far more immediate. Ownership is taken up in the hopes of a fast short-term profit. The swing trader does not buy stock because of an admiration for the company or its product; stock is merely the vehicle for creating those two- to five-day opportunities.

equity investment

a form of ownership in a corporation, the best-known form of which is stock.

So stock ownership is usually associated with taking an equity stake in the company, and the normal trading increment is 100 shares. This *round lot* is efficient because trading costs are tied to that number; buying fewer than 100 shares usually involves a higher cost-per-share to complete the transaction.

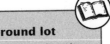

round lot
the usual trading increment for stocks, which is 100 shares.

A swing trader usually deals in rounds lots because of the trading cost of odd-lot trading. But were it possible to trade for the same costs, there is no doubt that swing traders would prefer a set *amount* over a fixed number of shares. That would allow the swing trader to quantify risk, spread capital more efficiently, and calculate potential profits. Many swing traders end up working only in stocks with relatively low price per share because capital is limited. This means that bigger point movement often seen in higher-priced stocks is another form of missed opportunity. You can actually set limits on each trade by finding appropriately priced options for one or more of a stable of stocks you track.

When you buy options instead of stock, capital limitations are not as much of an issue. As a general guideline, you can find and buy options at about 10 percent or less of the stock's current value. For example, you can find and buy options on a $60 stock for $600 or less. That $600 gives you complete control over the 100 shares of stock; fixes the price of the stock; and costs far less than outright purchase of 100 shares. This is the great advantage for swing traders.

With the use of stocks, you have to go either long or short; and short selling is where you run into risk issues and potentially unacceptable levels of loss. With options, you are either buy or sell into a position, make the swing trade, and act on both the buy and sell setup—all with limited risk and using long positions.

Key Point

When using options instead of round lots of stock for swing trading, you can have greater control over the dollar amount of each transaction—because your investment is based on option cost and not on share price.

call

an option granting its owner the right (but not the requirement) to buy 100 shares of a specific stock at a fixed price per share.

put

an option granting its owner the right (but not the requirement) to sell 100 shares of a specific stock at a fixed price per share.

expiration

the deadline for an option and the date on which it loses all of its value.

underlying stock

the stock on which options are written and bought or sold.

strike price

the fixed buy or sell price of stock specified in the option contract.

This is possible because there are two kinds of options, the *call* and the *put*. A call grants you the right (but not the requirement) to buy 100 shares of a specific stock at a fixed price per share; a put is the opposite, granting you the right to *sell* 100 shares of a specific stock at a fixed price per share. This arrangement remains in effect until *expiration* of the option.

However, it is crucial to remember that an option does not need to be used to buy or sell stock. Based on stock price changes, options gain or lose value; thus, options can themselves be bought and sold to create swing trading profits.

The option itself increases or decreases in value based on movement of the *underlying stock*, and this is where swing trading can use options to great advantage. The fixed price of the option is also called the *strike price* and it gives you the right to buy or sell 100 shares at that exact price, no matter how the market price of the stock changes. The farther the stock moves away from the strike price, the more the option value changes.

The value of the option, also called its *premium*, changes as the stock price moves, since the strike price is fixed. For example, if you purchase a 35 call, it means your strike price is $35 per share. So before expiration, if the stock were to rise to $42 per share, or seven points above the strike price, that call would have $700 of increased value above strike price. For the swing trader, this is the same as a seven-point rise in the stock—yet at a fraction of the cost and risk.

The situation works in reverse for the put. As a stock's value falls *below* the strike price of the put, the put's premium value grows. If you purchase a $35 put, for example, and the stock falls to $29 per share before expiration, the put's value grows six points, representing the price difference between $35 and $29 per share. The fact that calls and puts

---

Key Point

Options are specifically identified with individual stocks and with the price you can buy or sell shares of that stock. But option profits are not derived solely from buying or selling stock; because options gain or lose value—they can be traded on their own.

Key Point

When the stock moves in the desired direction (up when you own a call, or down when you own a put) the value of the option increases as well. So the option can be traded in place of stock. This is an incredible opportunity for swing traders.

---

grow in value based on stock price movement demonstrates the value of options to swing traders. You can trade in a much greater number of different stocks for less capital at risk.

The Status of Options

The option premium does not necessarily track the changes in stock value dollar for dollar. Actual movement of option premium value depends on the distance between current value and strike price, and on whether the strike price is higher or lower than market value. When an option is *at the money*, it means that the strike price of the option and market value of the stock are identical.

Options also have descriptive terms explaining where the strike price is in relation to current market value:

premium
the value or cost of an option, which varies according to the distance between strike price and current market value; and the time remaining until expiration.

at the money
a situation where an option's strike price is identical to the stock's current market value.

- When the call's strike price is below current market value of the stock, the call is *in the money*.

- When a put's strike price is above current market value of the stock, the put is in the money.

- When the call's strike price is above current market value of the stock, the call is *out of the money*.

- When the put's strike price is below current market value of the stock, the put is out of the money.

in the money

condition of an option when the strike price of a call is lower than current stock price, or when the strike price of a put is higher than the current stock price.

out of the money

condition of an option when the strike price of a call is higher than the current stock price, or when the strike price of a put is lower than the current stock price.

intrinsic value

the premium value of an option equal to the number of points it is in the money (current market value higher than a call's strike price or lower than a put's strike price).

A comparison of these situations is provided in Figure 8.1

The degree to which an option is in the money (strike price of the call is *lower* than current market value of the stock, or strike price of a put is *higher* than current market value of the stock) is where swing traders will find the most interesting attribute of options. The number of points in the money is referred to as *intrinsic value*. For example, if your call's strike price is 45 and the current market value of the stock is $48 per share, there are three points of intrinsic value in this option. The same works in the opposite direction for puts. If your put's strike price is 50 and the current market value of the stock is $46 per share, there are four points of intrinsic value in that put.

So if you have an in-the-money option, some portion of the premium represents intrinsic value. Any *additional* premium above and beyond intrinsic value is called *time value*. For example, if your call's strike price is 45 and the current market value of the stock is $48, but your call is current worth 5 ($500), that is made up of three points in intrinsic value and two points in time value. When an option is at the money or out of the money, the entire premium is made up of time value. The time value is going to be highest when a long time remains between today and expiration of the option.

Call

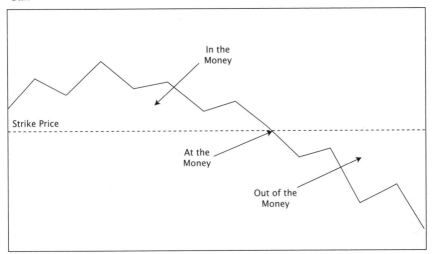

Put

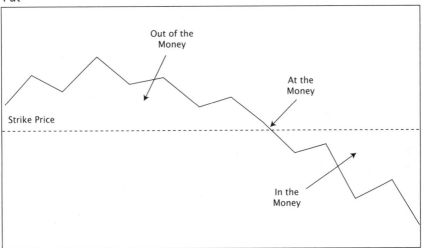

FIGURE 8.1   Call and Put: In and Out of the Money

Key Point

The in-the-money status is opposite for calls and for puts based on proximity to strike price. When strike price of the call is lower than market value, or when strike price of the put is higher, the option is in the money.

Key Point

The option consists of intrinsic value (equal to the number of points it is in the money) and time value. The time value is any value other than intrinsic value. When the option is at or out of the money, its premium is all time value.

---

time value
the portion of an option's premium excluding any intrinsic value.

Why is it important to know all of these terms? As a swing trader, you can capitalize on the cost of options, which is far lower than the underlying stock's price. It will be cheaper to buy options than it would be to buy shares of stock. Because each option gives you control over 100 shares, the lower cost of the option gives you considerable leverage, lower risk, and potentially greater return on your money. In order to effectively use options for swing trading, you will need to formulate an effective strategy with these important distinctions in mind (intrinsic and time value, in and out of the money, and expiration).

You have three primary advantages in swing trading with options. The attributes most important to remember include the following:

1. The option premium consists of both intrinsic value and time value. The intrinsic value equals the in-the-money point value, and time value decreases as expiration approaches.

2. In-the-money options change dollar for dollar with changes in the stock's value. When a call is in the money, the call's intrinsic value increases one point for each point the stock increases. When a put is in the money, the put's intrinsic value increases one point for each point the stock decreases.

3. Because time value declines as expiration approaches, options get cheaper toward the end of their terms.

A Realistic View of Time Value Premium

Just a profitability of buying and selling stock is often a matter of timing, option premium value also evolves and changes over time. The interesting aspect of options is that valuation of options is a combination of two factors: stock price movement and time.

The option premium consists of time value and intrinsic value. The intrinsic portion is easy to understand. It consists of the point value difference between strike price and current market value. When current market value is higher than a call's strike price, or lower than a put's strike price, the difference is intrinsic value. If the current market value of stock is lower than the call strike price or higher than the put strike price, there can be no intrinsic value. And the intrinsic value moves dollar for dollar with the stock price.

As far as intrinsic value is concerned, this is the key piece of information for swing traders. Knowing that in-the-money options move dollar for dollar with the stock, you can easily find the best options to use for swing trading.

With time value attributes brought into the equation, the selection of the best possible options might at first seem to become more difficult but in fact, it is easier. Most people who speculate in options face the ever-present problem of declining time value. When an option has a long time to go until expiration, its time value will be maximized. When expiration is going to arrive within a matter of a few weeks, time value declines rapidly. When expiration is only a few days away, time value falls to near zero.

Key Point

Swing traders are going to be most interested in tracking intrinsic value, which moves with the stock. This is where your profits will be found.

> ## Key Point
>
> You will notice that when option strike price is close to the current market value of the stock, they tend to be more responsive to price changes; and when farther away, increasingly less responsive.

To observe how time value acts and interacts with the stock price, it makes sense to watch options whose strike price is close to current market value. The farther away from market value, the less time value will respond to short-term price changes. Time value is more likely to relentlessly depreciate over time; and the closer expiration is, the more rapid the loss in time value. So, as many option speculators have discovered, buying options with too much time value can be a losing proposition, even if the stock price moves in the desired direction.

Let's say a stock sells today at $38 per share and you are thinking about buying a 40 call that expires in four months. The premium is 4 ($400). You believe strongly that this stock is going to see increased price value over the next four months, so buying the call seems like a wise idea. But because market value is lower than the call's strike price, there is no intrinsic value in this call; it is all time value.

You know that the time value will evaporate within the next four months, and will be at zero on the day of expiration. In order for this purchase to become profitable, you will need the stock to make a considerable move. If on the day of expiration, the stock's price were to rise to $44 per share, you would only break even (actually you would lose because this example does not consider trading costs for buying and for selling the call). This breakeven occurs because your original $400 cost (all time value) will have disappeared, and the intrinsic value (the difference between $44 per share market value and strike price of 40) would only replace that amount. So the call would still be worth only $400. This demonstrates why about three-fourths of all options expire worthless. Buying time value options is a difficult way to make money consistently. You have to fight not only the chance that the stock's price might move in the wrong direction, but time as well.

This is where options become too risky for most people. Buying options with a large portion of time value (or, as in the example, with no intrinsic value) is quite difficult. If the stock does not accumulate intrinsic value quickly, the purchase is not going to be profitable. This is true even if the stock were to move upward very quickly when still four months away from expiration. For example, what if you bought the 40 call when the stock was at $38 per share and, the very next day, the stock jumped to $40 per share? Would you expect the option to also jump two points?

Remember, intrinsic value tracks the stock dollar for dollar, so any growth above strike price level would create intrinsic value; and that is good news. However, the time value (100 percent of the premium at or below the 40 strike level) is time value and it will not react on a point-for-point level. Because the two-point move places the stock right at the money, the option premium might grow to a degree, but it probably will not increase by two points. You need to see the stock move into the in-the-money range before a point-for-point change will begin to occur.

This brings up another aspect of time value premium: It is not strictly related to time. The major effect of time value premium is time, of course. But this premium is also affected by two additional elements: investor interest, and proximity. Investor interest is seen in volume increasing, in the stock's price rising, and in exceptionally high volatility. So the more volatile the stock becomes, the greater the likelihood that time value will increase above other stocks with lower volatility. Second, as the current market value of a stock approaches the strike price, time value premium is more likely to be responsive. Therefore when a stock is within one or two points of strike price, the option premium may anticipate the possibility of its moving into the intrinsic range, and this may create more responsiveness in the time value premium. This means (1) for calls the stock price would be within close range just below strike price and (2) for puts the stock price would be just above strike price.

Key Point

Time value is not strictly related to time. It is also affected by investor interest and by proximity between strike price and current market value of the stock.

extrinsic value

the value of an option not counting any intrinsic value; the time value premium, given this alternate name to consider the non-time elements of volatility within the stock, and of proximity between stock's current market value and the option's strike price.

Thus the market interest and proximity to strike price make "time value" more complex than a predictable time measurement. Time value premium varies from one stock to another and, because time is not the only factor influencing the option premium, time value is more accurately described as *extrinsic value*.

A Strategic Approach to Swing Trading

The problem for swing traders in the selection and use of options is based entirely on the time value premium and how it behaves. If you attempt to swing trade with options containing a large portion of time value, you will spend less for the options, but you face a more serious problem: Option premium will not change or move in the same way that the stock's price changes and moves.

With this in mind, swing traders need to develop some standards for the use of options. The standards should consider two goals: optimizing intrinsic value. These standards should include:

1. *Use only those options that are in the money.* Swing traders need the point-for-point interaction between option premium and stock price. In-the-money options have intrinsic value, and that portion of the option premium will rise or fall point for point in tracking the stock. So when you see the buy or sell setup, you can respond using long position options. Rather than going long or short in the stock, you can buy calls for buy setups and buy puts for short setups.

Key Point

Swing traders using options have to contend with the cost of time value versus the actual amount of time to expiration.

Key Point

In-the-money options are the only practical ones for swing traders to use. You *need* the responsiveness of intrinsic value to make the strategy work.

This gives you numerous advantages over going long or short in stock. The cost of buying options is significantly less than that for buying stock. On the short side, the cost factor affects you as well, since margin requirement demands that you place at least 50 percent of the stock's value on margin when you sell stock short. With options, the cost will average 10 percent of the stock price. This 10 percent is not a hard-and-fast rule, but an analysis of actual option premium values on various stocks reveals that the cost may even be far less.

2. *Limit swing trading options to those as close as possible to strike price.* The biggest problem in buying options for swing trading involves paying for time value. But fortunately, when expiration date is quite near, time value is reduced to an absolute minimum. This is especially true when the intrinsic value of options is quite close to the strike price. If you are responding to a buy setup, look for calls that are in the money but also within five to 10 points below current market value. That provides the least amount of time value for the smallest cost.

Although time value may be a factor when the strike price is close to current market value of the stock, it is minimal when

Key Point

Work with options that are in the money and as close as possible to current market value. This gives you the most responsive price action for the least cost.

expiration will occur within the near future. While most option speculators consider pending expiration a problem, swing traders do not because they intend to hold positions open only for the short term. This raises an issue of risk as well. When you go long on stock or sell short, you assume a market risk equal to the potential change in a stock value. For example, if you buy shares at $55 and the market value falls to $48 per share, you lose $7 per share, or $700 on a 100-share trade. When you go short, you have the same risk. If a stock's price rises four points, your 100 short shares are worth $400 more, and you will have to pay that to close the position. But with options, your maximum risk is always limited to the cost of the option. When you assume a long position in either calls or puts, the most you can ever loose is the premium amount you pay upon opening that position.

Swing traders do have losses, just as all traders and investors. So swing trading is a timing strategy intended to improve your odds and to increase profitability in trading. However, the market risk cannot be ignored and losses are painful. For short sellers, the potential losses are unknown so many swing traders simply avoid the short side. Options solve the market risk problem by limiting losses to the cost of the options. And using options for swing trading also limits the possible losses from both long and short positions in stock. Because options cost only a fraction of stock purchases, you can also diversify your swing trades among many more stocks than you could buying or going short on 100-share increments.

3. *Avoid long-term options and use only those that will expire within the next month.* While most option buyers have to struggle to offset option cost with time, as a swing trader you are not concerned with time windows beyond the usual two- to five-day window. This means that you can deal strictly with options that will expire within the next month's cycle. If you buy calls and puts that expire within the next four weeks or less (close to strike price and in the money) the risks are manageable. As long as the majority of your swing trade setup signals are accurate, you will be in and out of the position in less than one week. In those situations where you lose money, your loss will be limited to the cost of the option.

Key Point

Limit swing trading to only those options that expire within the next month. Swing trading is short-term, so why pay for time value?

That cost is held down by two important aspects. First, there is virtually no time value to contend with because expiration is imminent and the closer the time to expiration, the less time value will remain. Second, because the option will be as close as possible to strike price, intrinsic value will be very low. For example, if your call is three points below strike price, intrinsic value will be only 3 ($300). And if your put is two points above strike price, intrinsic value will be only 2 ($200).

Examples of Options for Swing Trading

Is it possible to locate low-cost calls or puts close to expiration and within a few points of strike price? Yes. In fact, these selection criteria are normally the most affordable options for swing trading. For speculative purposes, out-of-the-money options are much cheaper; but as a swing trader, you need and want the point-for-point price movement typical of intrinsic value. Some examples:

		Calls		*Puts*	
Stock and Trading Symbol	*Market Value*	*Expiration*	*Value*	*Expiration*	*Value*
Sherwin-Williams (SHW)	$50.31	Aug 45	$5.30	Aug 55	$4.80
Procter & Gamble (PG)	56.56	Aug 50	6.70	Aug 60	3.60
Johnson & Johnson (JNJ)	62.67	Aug 60	2.95	Aug 65	2.40

> ## Key Point
>
> Option notation involves a dollars-and-cents expression for a single share of stock, but this has to be multiplied by 100, since each option involves right for 100 shares. For example, an option worth 5 sells for $500.

To interpret these results accurately, the call and put values are per-share values, so to calculate the contract cost, they must be multiplied by 100. The method by which option premium values are shown in listings is using this method. So a call listed with a value of $5.30 will cost you $530. As a swing trader, you may be able to recognize the value in using options rather than shares of stock as soon as these values are compared. The following is a summary of the call or put costs compared to the cost of buying 100 shares in each case:

Stock and Trading Symbol	Market Value	Cost of 100 Shares	Cost per Option
Sherwin-Williams (SHW)	$50.31	$5,031	
Aug 45 call $5.30			$530
Aug 55 put $4.80			480
Procter & Gamble (PG)	56.56	$5,656	
Aug 50 call $6.70			$670
Aug 60 put $3.60			360
Johnson & Johnson (JNJ)	62.67	$6,267	
Aug 60 call $2.95			$295
Aug 65 put $2.40			240

These comparisons demonstrate the value of using options rather than buying 100 shares (on the buy setup) or going short 100 shares (on the sell setup). When you consider the return on your investment, the difference is even more significant. For example, a three-point move on the buy setup for each of these stocks looks like this (without including transaction costs):

Sherwin-Williams (SHW)

100 shares of stock, $200 profit ($200 ÷ $5,031) =   4.0%

1 August 45 call, $200 profit ($200 ÷ $530) =   37.7

Procter & Gamble (PG)

100 shares of stock, $200 profit ($200 ÷ $5,656) =   3.5%

1 August 45 call, $200 profit ($200 ÷ $670) =   29.9

Johnson & Johnson (JNJ)

100 shares of stock, $200 profit ($200 ÷ $6,267) =   3.0%

1 August 45 call, $200 profit($200 ÷ $295) =   67.8

For a sell setup, using long puts instead of selling short 100 shares of stock, and assuming a two-point move on the trade, the comparison looks like this:

Sherwin-Williams (SHW)

100 shares of stock, $200 profit ($200 ÷ $5,031) =   4.0%

1 August 55 call, $200 profit ($200 ÷ $480) =   41.7

Procter & Gamble (PG)

100 shares of stock, $200 profit ($200 ÷ $5,656) =   3.5%

1 August 60 call, $200 profit ($200 ÷ $360) =   55.6

Johnson & Johnson (JNJ)

100 shares of stock, $200 profit ($200 ÷ $6,267) =   3.0%

1 August 65 call, $200 profit ($200 ÷ $240) =   83.3

A two-point move in the option therefore produces a double-digit return in each of these examples. It works with calls in the buy setup and it works with long puts in the sell setup. Assuming you select stocks with adequate midrange volatility, swing trades will be practical. All three of these stocks qualify as reasonable swing trading candidates.

Figure 8.2 shows a 30-day chart for Sherwin-Williams. Note that at point 1 there is an apparent reversal signal. After four downtrend days, a

---

Key Point

Clearly, you will only want to swing trade using options on stocks which provide clear buy or sell setup signals. The difference is that instead of buying or selling stock, you either buy calls (for buy setups) or buy puts (for sell setups).

---

narrow range day on the upside appears. This is confirmed two days later with a strong engulfing line day. The stock then rose five points to the end of the chart. The comparisons of stock prices to option values were provided for the day on which this chart ended.

The case is strong but not as strong for Procter & Gamble. Figure 8.3 shows the 30-day period preceding the day on which stock and option values were shown. The large engulfing line at point # 1 foretold a two-point rise in the stock's market value. The smaller engulfing line day

FIGURE 8.2 30-Day Chart: Sherwin-Williams
Source: Candlestickchart.com.

at point 2 preceded a one-point drop in value. (Recalling that the PG put produced a 55.6 percent return on a two-point move, it is reasonable to assume that a corresponding put move at this point would have easily yielded 25 percent or more.)

Finally, Figure 8.4 summarizes the 30 days preceding the previous example for Johnson & Johnson. Here a narrow range day at point 1 followed three down days and accurately anticipated a three-point uptrend in the stock, to the end of the chart. At that point, a narrow range day provides a sell setup after an extended uptrend on the day the stock and option values were shown.

The usual problem for option buyers is the double issue of declining time value and pending expiration. These two factors make it quite difficult to simply buy and sell options as a speculative market play. Even though the relatively low cost of options is attractive at first glance, it may be quite deceptive as well. The majority of first-time option buyers lose more than they earn in option outcomes.

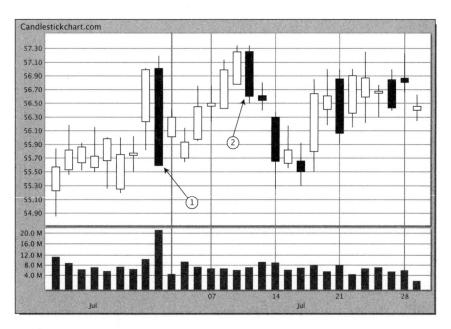

FIGURE 8.3 30-Day Chart: Procter & Gamble
Source: Candlestickchart.com.

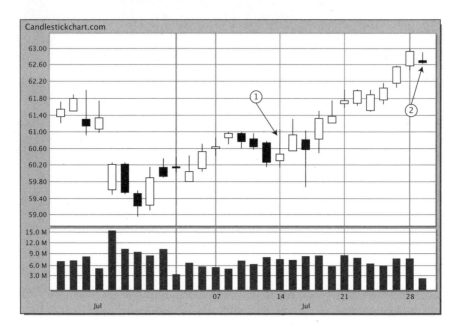

FIGURE 8.4   30-Day Chart: Johnson & Johnson
Source: Candlestickchart.com.

Swing traders make use of options as a device for achieving the same outcome as they do using shares of stock. The significant differences, though, include two primary points:

1. *Better return on the investment.* The previous example makes the point that options yield far better swing trading returns. In fact, using options vastly changes the landscape for swing trading. Most investors will have to view swing trading from the point of view that capital is limited. Even using a 50 percent margin limitation, you cannot take part in very many swing trades at the same time. A portfolio of $10,000 will enable you to buy 100 shares each of Sherwin-Williams, Procter & Gamble and Johnson & Johnson, or go short on 100 shares of each (or a combination of each), using the 50 percent margin allowance the rules allow. But that would be *all* you could do with $10,000.

    In comparison, you could buy or sell as many as 400 calls or puts with the same $10,000 without using the margin account at all. If you compare the use of 100-share increments of stock to

---

Key Point

The double-digit returns possible on swing trading with options are compelling reasons to prefer short-term options over shares of stock.

1-contract options, it is clear that swing trading strategies can be vastly expanded. For example, you could buy single options on 400 different stocks; or 40 groups of 10-option contracts on 25 different stocks. That raises your potential profits considerably. With 10-option groups, your transaction costs will be lower on a per-contract basis, while potential profits will be vastly improved. Options give you not only a better return on your investment, but much better diversification as well.

2. *Much lower market risk in terms of dollars invested.* The problem in using shares of stock for swing trading is that it involves market risks on both sides. Buying 100 shares of stock in groups of $5,000 or more at a time is risky because if the stock's price falls, you lose money—possibly a large portion of your money. With a call, however, your maximum loss is limited to the premium for the call. In the three-stock example, the closest calls to strike prices cost only a fraction of the stock value for each case.

On the short setup side, you will be required to go short on the stock. If your timing is off or the sell setup was simply inaccurate and the stock rises, you would need to buy out the position at a loss or continue placing more and more money on margin to keep your ratio with the

---

Key Point

Risks are much lower using in-the-money options for two reasons. First, you can never lose more than the option premium. Second, you never have to sell short.

---

brokerage firm. Short selling is complex and risky. In comparison, when you buy a put you are going long to respond to the sell setup, an elegant solution to the problem of short-side risk. The most you can lose is the premium value of the put. In the three-stock example, put premium ranged from $240 to $480, a small portion of the stocks whose price per 100 shares was between 10 and 26 times higher than using puts.

Swing Trading for Options Speculators

Another aspect of this to consider is that, from the option speculator's point of view, swing trading can be viewed as a method for timing long options. The dilemma most novices face is deciding how much to pay and how far out to go with options. The cost factor is ever present; option speculators naturally want to find the most attractive option bargains with the greatest time to expiration. But the longer the time, the higher the time value will be.

For example, consider the further-out options for the previous examples:

Sherwin-Williams

Aug 45 call	*$5.30*	*Aug 55 put*	*$4.80*
Sep 45 call	6.00	Sep 55 put	5.10
Dec 45 call	7.10	Dec 55 put	5.90
Jan 45 call	7.60	Jan 55 put	6.10

Procter & Gamble

Aug 50 call	*$6.70*	*Aug 60 put*	*$3.60*
Oct 50 call	7.20	Oct 60 put	4.00
Jan 50 call	7.90	Jan 50 put	5.50

Johnson & Johnson

Aug 60 call	*$2.95*	*Aug 65 put*	*$2.40*
Sep 60 call	3.10	Sep 65 put	2.80
Oct 60 call	3.70	Oct 65 put	3.00
Jan 60 call	4.70	Jan 65 put	3.50

The longer out these options go until expiration, the higher the time value. Those that expire the soonest (italicized) have very little time value, which is what makes them most attractive for swing trading; those going out five months have far more time value. So from the point of view of the option speculator, this is a dilemma. Do you pay $100 to $200 more for an option and buy time? Or do you buy options with almost no time value and hope for a strong price movement within a few weeks?

An option speculator is continually seeking bargains and opportunities and, most of the time, not being able to profit from long position options. Based on the volume of option trades, it is also clear that traders prefer calls over puts. This may be true because investors tend to be optimists, and will think about options only in terms of stock prices rising, rarely in terms of those prices falling. So like swing traders who do not want to short stock, option traders who look only to calls miss half their potential market.

Table 8.1 summarizes call and put activity for 20 stocks in a single month, which makes this point. It seems to not matter that many of the stocks whose call volume was a clear majority, actually fell in value. The fact remains that most option traders prefer calls over puts.

Key Point

Options make a lot of sense for swing traders. And for the same reasons, the clarity in setup signals for swing trading could make it a valuable strategy for option speculators and traders.

Key Point

Most people prefer to think stocks are going to rise in the near future. This explains why calls outsell puts. But as every swing trader knows, stocks rise and fall in predictable patterns. Calls *and* puts are equally valuable.

| | Call | Total | |
Company Name	Volume	Volume	Call
Altria	519,468	795,552	65%
Microsoft	428,122	706,904	61%
General Motors	203,291	651,568	31%
Sprint	114,490	588,158	19%
Apple Computer	357,361	572,880	23%
Google	313,144	563,112	56%
Intel	350,788	497,960	70%
Hewlett-Packard	215,526	365,752	59%
General Electric	200,276	294,440	68%
Chevron	182,352	276,798	66%
Exxon Mobil	165,992	275,678	60%
ConocoPhillips	191,329	252,635	76%
Newmont Mining	124,012	242,625	51%
Pfizer	136,031	236,711	57%
Goldman Sachs	145,626	229,432	63%
Yahoo	147,654	220,701	67%
Bank of America	95,123	215,326	44%
Wal-Mart	130,971	211,941	62%
JPMorgan Chase	115,831	201,297	58%
Citigroup	120,952	194,443	62%
Total	4,258,339	7,593,913	
Average			56%

TABLE 8.1 Put Activity for 20 Stocks in a Single Month

The next chapter expands on this discussion to demonstrate how swing traders can employ some specific strategies using options—not only to reduce losses, but also to improve on gains.

Option Strategies for Swing Trading

The potential uses of options are richly varied. They can be employed as high-risk, very speculative, and leveraged plays; or they can be used as an ultra-conservative method for building income in a methodical manner. Swing traders at all risk levels can make good use of options as a smart alternative to the expensive strategy of buying shares of stock in round lots, or the high-risk strategy of shorting stock.

Swing trading as a strategic approach to short-term trading opens up many possibilities—however, by using stocks, it also comes with severe disadvantages. Specifically, these include limitations on how much swing trading can be done because capital is limited; and the serious levels of risk in using stock, especially selling short. So options solve these problems—as long as you use only long strategies such as buying calls for buy setups and buying puts for sell setups. However, many additional, advanced strategies are also possible using options.

It is important to recognize exactly how calls and puts work as swing trading devices. The call is a substitute for buying shares of stock, and each call grants you the rights to 100 shares of stock. This means you can buy 100 shares at a fixed price before expiration, or you can sell the call at a profit (this is what swing traders are most likely to do). A put is more confusing. When you buy a put, you are taking up a long position, but it acts as a substitute for selling 100 shares of stock. The put grants

---

Key Point

Options can be used in a large array of different low-risk and high-risk configurations. For swing traders, options can be the ideal vehicle.

---

you the right to sell 100 shares at a fixed price before expiration. So once you own the call, you could exercise it and sell 100 shares at a price higher than current market value; or, as a swing trader, you can sell the put at a profit following a downtrend.

With these basics in place, you can expand your use of options beyond their use as buy or sell setup responses. You can do more with options within your swing trading strategy.

Strategic Considerations and Risk

The use of options has to be studied in terms of risk, because—as with all strategies—the ultimate success or failure depends on whether it is appropriate for you. Every trader is willing to accept some risk, but how much? For some, swing trading using any method is simply too risky, especially if your orientation is toward a buy-and-hold preference with well-established, low-volatility companies. If this describes you as an investor, then swing trading will not be considered seriously as an alternative. Neither will options.

Some traders are willing to take higher risks and even highly speculative risks. The idea is that if an exceptionally high profit is possible, it justifies the equal possibility of a complete loss. Such a speculator may find swing trading too methodical, too low-risk, and—even with options—not profitable enough.

Somewhere in between these extremes are most traders. A starting point for anyone considering using options as a swing trading device needs to identify their appropriate risk level. Most people will be far more comfortable staying on the long side of transactions than on the short side, so options certainly double up your trading opportunities. One possibility in devising your own swing trading strategy is to buy shares of stock for buy-in signals, but to use puts for sell setups. This keeps you away from short selling of stock. However, it does require buying either round lots of shares, or paying higher trading fees for odd-lot purchases of stock. It begs this question if you intend to keep swing trade positions open for only a two- to five-day window: Why not use options on both sides of the transaction?

One of the primary advantages in using options rather than stocks is the leverage they provide. This is a feature swing traders have to put high on their list. The comparison has been provided in the last chapter, but it bears emphasizing again here. Option cost is a fraction of stock cost, and yet each option contract produces the same profit as 100 shares of stock. For example, if you are comparing a $50 stock to an option on that stock at 10 percent of the stock's price, and your swing trade produces a three-point profit:

	Stock	*Option*
Initial investment	$5,000	$500
Three-point move	300	300
Value excluding brokerage fees	$5,300	$800
Return on investment	6%	60%

The rate of return is higher, *and* the capital at risk is lower. Now consider what happens if you hold the stock for a period of time equal to the time to go until option expiration, and the option expires worthless. The most you lose on the option is $500. With a $5,000 investment in stock, your potential loss is far greater. If the stock falls eight points, your paper loss would be $800. If it fell 12 points, your loss would be $1,200. So leverage, combined with the limitation on potential loss, makes a great difference in the use of options for swing trading.

The combined point of view should allow for the pro and con of the option as an alternative to buying and selling shares. The leverage factor should be the strongest of all considerations, even if the market risk is discounted. Most traders object to options for several reasons, including:

1. *Expiration factor.* The fact that options expire at some point in the future is troubling for many. This would be a key problem if it were merely a matter of speculating on option values, but swing traders expect (and want) a fast turnaround in their transactions. That two- to five-day window makes options the perfect alternative to buying and selling stock. The lack of time value in extremely short-term contracts is an advantage, because the majority of intrinsic-value premium will track stock values exactly.

2. *Exotic reputation.* Options have always been thought of as high-risk, very exotic instruments. Many serious traders with considerable market experience reject options out of hand based on only a partial knowledge of how the options market works and on risk level perceptions, which may also be false. In fact, options are exotic in the sense that they are not tangible, have no specific equity, and are strange and foreign to traditional thinking; but they are not high-risk. In fact, swing traders *reduce* their risks in the use of options, while expanding their field of play.

Key Point

Expiration is a problem for most long option positions. For swing trading, however, pending expiration is not a problem because it is preferable to buy options with little or not time value.

Key Point

Most people consider *all* options to be high-risk. When properly used, however, options fill a wide range of needs—from speculative to ultraconservative.

3. *Knowledge and experience.* The fear factor dominates most trader objections to options. The lack of specific knowledge, coupled with the negative reputation that options have in the equity markets, explains why so many people want nothing to do with this market. Some well-publicized abuses among speculators and hedge funds have only bolstered the negative reputation of the options market. But in fact, swing traders do not need to live with those high-risk strategies associated with short-side option plays, or with excessive long position uses involving long shots. They can devise a strategy that is not only low-risk and even conservative in many instances; and avoid the high risk of the wilder, more commonly held view of options.

4. *Traditional preference for equity position.* The intangible nature of options is also troubling to anyone who has not actively traded in the past. Traders, even with limitations of capital for swing trading, are likely to feel more comfortable owning shares than owning options in their place. On the short side, it becomes a struggle between risks. Short selling stock is risky and demands margin levels be maintained; in comparison, long puts are fairly inexpensive and risks are limited. However, overcoming the traditional preference to the desire for stock *ownership* is a large obstacle.

Key Point

No strategy should be employed unless you thoroughly understand the risks. This demands experience and knowledge as a first step.

Key Point

A common bias against options is their intangible nature. Investors like equity positions. But as a swing trader, it is worth looking beyond this bias since, even when trading with stock, the goal is not to accumulate equity but to produce income.

> ### Key Point
>
> Some people view short selling as sophisticated and high-level in terms of investor "smarts." In fact, you reduce risks when you use long puts instead of shorting stock, and it requires much less capital.

5. *Attraction to short selling.* Even though short selling is quite risky and thus problematical for most people, there is a certain attraction to it that cannot be ignored. The idea of selling short is associated with sophisticated investors who somehow know more than the average investor. This perception is quite real, but dangerous. There is nothing especially sophisticated about short selling, especially when you compare its features to buying puts. Although puts expire, the risks of remaining in a short position for stock over an extended period of time are significant. Just as people are attracted to sophisticated investing (including not only short selling, but buying tax-free bonds, futures, and index funds, for example), there may be a certain appeal. Yet those choices are not always appropriate in terms of knowledge, experience, tax status, or investing goals. By the same argument, you may avoid short selling if the risks are far too great for you. Using put options as an alternative solves many problems.

Stock Selection versus Options

Swing trading is going to depend on the movement and change in stock prices. Even if you end up trading options on a stock, you will continue to rely on setup in the stock price to time your trades. This is true because option premium levels may change in ways separate from stock prices. Time value itself—the portion not specifically restricted to time, but including proximity and investor interest—can and does move in ways not related to actual changes in the stock itself.

So, if your swing trading strategy involves the use of options, you will do best when you track the stock and make decisions based on setup trends; and then make your trades using the related options. The guidelines continue to apply: The options you pick should be short-term, as close as possible to strike price, and in the money.

The question of how to pick stocks for swing trading should depend on the same criteria as you use when your strategy involves buying or selling shares. Picking swing trade stocks based on the relative value of options is a mistake. Option pricing reflects varying degrees of change in time value premium or, to be more precise, extrinsic value of those options. Because this value has nothing to do with the relationship between stock market value and option premium value, it is dangerous to pick stocks based on option values. The extrinsic valuation of options relates more to investor perceptions about companies than actual value.

If you go back to swing trading basics, you will recall that swing trading is a method for capitalizing on the emotions that rule the market: greed, fear and uncertainty. The cool-headed swing trader, recognizing which emotion is ruling at the moment, times trades to profit from the emotional over-reaction between buyers and sellers. So variations in an option's extrinsic value have to be viewed as yet another aspect of this same phenomenon. The market is ruled by emotions, which are seen in short-term stock price movement *and* in the distortion of option premium value.

This is a profound bit of market intelligence. The emotional actions and reactions of the market are not limited to stock prices, but include option premium value as well. Intrinsic value is an absolute, representing one point for each point in the money. Time value or, more accurately, extrinsic value is far more complex *and* troubling for you as a swing trader. This is why it is so important to remember the guideline: Track stock prices but trade options.

Key Point

Just as emotions rule the markets in short-term stock price movement, they also affect extrinsic value of options. Knowing this gives you a great advantage in using options for swing trading.

Nothing changes as far as following trends and looking for buy and sell setups. The only difference is the use of long calls in place of long stock; and the use of long puts in place of short stock.

Option traders eventually learn that simply picking options to buy or sell is an expensive approach to the market. They are better off picking stocks based on sound analysis and comparison of risks. The same rule applies to swing traders. The decision about which stocks to include or exclude should be based on a traditional analysis of a range of stocks, and development of a short list of criteria. These should include position of the company within its stock sector; capital strength; and profitability. You may pick specific ratios such as the P/E to further narrow your list, or restrict your selection to those stocks paying higher than average dividends. These are simply examples of methods you can use to narrow your list of likely swing trading stocks from thousands, down to less than 20 stocks. If you go long or short in stocks, you are likely to be able to swing trade in only a handful of stocks; with options, you can easily consider a range of 20 stocks and perhaps even more.

You may also use technical considerations to pick appropriate stocks. The criteria for swing trading are a good match for options criteria. Technical analysis includes comparisons of the trading range and historical volatility; you need and want stocks that are moderately volatile to create strong setup signals for swing trading. Those same stocks also tend to exhibit a healthy range of options and premium values.

However, one thing is sure about time value. When the option is within two to four weeks of expiration, the time value premium rapidly declines to zero. This occurs even when the extrinsic factors remain in play. So investor interest and proximity between strike price and market value may play a role right up to the week preceding expiration; but from your swing trading point of view, expiration will ultimately mean that the option premium is going to consist primarily of intrinsic value.

Key Point

You need to divide time value into two components: time itself and other extrinsic factors. It is certain, however, that as expiration nears all forms of non-intrinsic value will evaporate from the option premium.

To get an idea of how critical the timing of expiration is, review some option listings that are about to expire. Even those with strike prices within a few points of market value will have very little value right before expiration, often only 0.05, which is five dollars. This is only a token value serving the purpose of giving some minimal value to the option because it remains alive, if only for a few days. Few speculators will invest in such options because they are about to expire and they are out of the money. It is certainly possible that the stock will surge in the last minute and the option will move suddenly in the money, creating some last-minute profit. This is the exception rather than the rule. From a swing trading perspective, even in-the-money options on the verge of expiration have very little time value remaining. This is your great advantage. By limiting your swing trading to the appropriate placed options, you pay primarily for that intrinsic value, and you are more likely to see the point-for-point movement in value that makes options so desirable for swing trading.

Swing Trading with Multiple-Option Contracts

The most obvious and immediate advantage to trading multiple option contracts is the savings in brokerage fees. For example, Charles Schwab & Company (http://www.schwab.com) charges $9.95 per trade plus 75 cents per contract for online options trades. So a single option costs $10.70; two options cost $11.45; and 10 options traded at the same time cost $17.45, or less than $1.75 per contract.

The savings are only the first and most obvious type of economy. Multiple contracts also add great flexibility to your swing trading strategy. Multiple contract strategies may include:

1. *Partial profit-taking, partial hold.* You can add great flexibility to your swing trading strategy when you employ multiple contracts. For example, you may respond to a buy setup by going long on four calls for a stock. After an exceptionally strong uptrend, you can close out the position at a profit. Or, as an alternative, if you expect the momentum to carry the stock even higher, you can close out two of the calls, covering your cost and producing a profitable result; and hold onto the remaining two calls. For example, the 60-day chart for Diebold (DBD) provides an example of momentum in both directions, as shown in Figure 9.1

Key Point

You can tie in profits with multiple options by closing some positions and keeping others open. When trend turns to momentum, this creates much greater profits.

FIGURE 9.1   60-Day Chart with Momentum in Both Directions: Diebold
Source: Candlestickchart.com.

The movement in this stock showed momentum in both directions, the first three in downtrends and the final in an uptrend. In this situation, a swing trade using multiple contracts could have produced additional profits due to the momentum trend. You could, for example, have reacted to the sell setup at the very beginning of the chart by buying four puts. The downtrend appeared to end at note 1. However, the downtrend was quite strong and in only five days produced a five-point fall in the stock's price. If it were possible to cover your investment and produce a profit by selling two of the puts and continuing to hold the remaining two, you could have gained an additional point of profit by observing the sell setup at note 2, or the other at point

3. You may have also noted the buy setup at the extremely narrow spinning top signaling the bottom of the downtrend. At that point the remaining two puts could have been closed out and even replaced with the purchase of four calls (in response to the strong buy signal). While the sell signal occurred nine days later, the uptrend was strong; so you could have sold two of the calls and held the remaining calls to ride out the upward momentum in the stock.

This example provides a clear view of how you can modify your swing trading strategy with a multiple option approach. At those times when the trend is especially strong (either upward or downward), it makes sense first to cover your investment and produce a small profit; and second to continue holding through the momentum to produce additional profits.

2. *Partial profit-taking, partial exercise.* Some swing traders decide that they want to buy and keep shares of a particular stock. One form of diversification that makes a lot of sense is to identify hold stocks and invest in them; and also swing trade on the short-term price changes in the same stock. The traditional method for buying stocks is acceptable for this, of course. However, so many opportunities are lost because investors hesitate. Options can solve this problem as part of a swing trading strategy.

For example, you may identify a limited number of stocks that you believe would provide worthwhile long-term investments as well as profitable swing trade candidates. On a buy signal, you purchase four calls and the strong moves upward strongly. At this point, many swing traders face a dilemma. If you swing trade using stocks, do you sell shares after the uptrend and take profits?

Key Point

For anyone combining swing trading with a long-term hold strategy, options enable you to pursue both strategies in the same trades. This gives you far greater flexibility than a complete separation of strategies.

Or if the stock will continue to rise, should you just hold onto those shares? In many respects, the goals of long-term investing and swing trading contradict one another. However, using calls you can accomplish the goals of both strategies: profiting from short-term upswings *and* creating discount basis in stocks.

This is the result of selling two of the calls to take profits at the top of the upswing; and exercising the remaining two calls to purchase 200 shares below current market value. At this point, if you also believe that a sell setup has occurred in the stock's price, you can also purchase puts as part of your on-going swing trading strategy. That creates two strategic advantages. First is the swing trade setup; second is the downside protection it provides for your long-term stock investment. Every loss in the stock will be offset by gains in the puts. If you buy two puts and hold 200 shares, the offset is equal. If you buy four puts per 200 shares, your swing trading profit on a downtrend will be *double* the loss in the long stock.

A six-month chart for Anheuser-Busch (BUD) demonstrates how this works out. The chart is shown in Figure 9.2.

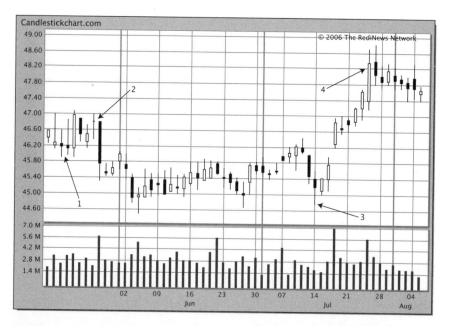

FIGURE 9.2   Swing Trading Profit on Downtrend: Anheuser-Busch
Source: Candlestickchart.com.

At note 1, a buy setup occurs. At this point, you could purchase four calls in the stock. By point 2, you may determine that the swing trading upswing is exhausted; however, you also believe the long-term prospects for this stock make it a worthwhile buy. So you cover your investment by selling two calls and exercising the remaining two, buying 200 shares. Because a sell signal has occurred, you also buy four puts. The stock immediately falls nearly two points. However, your swing traded four puts would have increased by twice the amount of the loss in the 200 shares. The puts could be closed out profitably at any time in the "uncertainty" range of trading that dominates the middle section of the chart.

A similar pattern emerged at point 3. Here a clear buy setup occurred, so you may have purchased four calls at about the 45 level. Note the price gap taking place three days later on a strong uptrend. That uptrend continued through eight days in total. At point 4, a sell setup appeared. The stock peaked at nearly $49 per share. You could sell all of the calls and take a nice swing trading profit; or you could sell two of the calls and cover your position, and exercise the remaining two. Exercise would get you 200 shares at $45 per share at a point where the stock was trading between $48 and $49.

3. *Incremental additions to momentum situations.* Referring once again to Figure 9.2, another swing trading strategy involves the use of multiple contracts when a trend shows momentum. For example, the price gap occurring right after note 3 shows a strong upward trend. If you had picked up calls at the buy setup at note 3, you could buy additional calls at any time during the eight-day uptrend, ultimately closing the position upon seeing the sell setup at note 4.

Key Point

Buying long-position stock or increasing short-position stock is expensive and high-risk. But with options, it is an affordable and often viable strategy to increase open positions based on price trends.

This example demonstrates that swing trading does not have to consist of a single opening position and a single closing position. You can modify your positions at any time. Using stock on either long or short side, this can become quite expensive; but option brokerage fees are so low that you have much greater flexibility to modify positions. Figure 9.2 shows a good example of how incremental additions can be made to augment your swing trading profits.

Covered Calls and Swing Trading

The use of multiple options in a swing trading strategy provides you with great flexibility, while enabling you to invest far less capital. Because options cost only a fraction of stock, you can afford to use multiple contracts, improving the potential for much greater profits as well. Because swing trades often involve only a point or two of price movement, multiple contracts make sense. If you open a swing trading position, for example, with 100 shares of stock, a one-half point change in price barely covers your transaction fees. Yet if you purchase four options instead, a one-half point change in the right price direction is the same as a two-point move for 100 shares of stock.

The potential for profits with reduced risks is even greater if you swing trade on stocks you already own. The *covered call* is a way to go short using options, but without the significant risks that involves when you don't own 100 shares per option contract.

covered call

an option strategy in which a call is sold, but the seller also owns 100 shares of the stock. In the event the call is exercised, the 100 shares are used to satisfy the call.

A covered call is so named because you own 100 shares of stock for each call sold. So the market risk is protected by the ownership of those shares. For example, you buy 100 shares of stock and sell a call. If the buyer on the other side exercises, you are required to deliver 100 shares at the strike price. The risk is eliminated entirely because you have the shares. A covered call makes sense when the net investment in 100 shares of stock is lower than the strike price. So if you buy stock at $52 per share and sell a 55 call, this exercise would produce $55 per share, a profit of three dollars per share. In addition, you keep the premium you are paid when you sell the call.

Key Point

Properly placed, the covered call is one of the most conservative strategies you can use in the market, whether as a swing trading strategy or simply as a method for increasing current income and discounting your basis in stock.

The risk is virtually eliminated as long as you own shares. In comparison, an *uncovered call* is extremely risky. Also called a *naked call*, this is a short position opened when you do not own 100 shares of stock. It is possible that the stock's price could rise significantly, creating a large loss. When an uncovered call is exercised, the seller is required to deliver 100 shares at the strike price. So if you sell an uncovered call at 55 and the stock rises to $62 per share, the call will be exercised; and you will lose $700 ($62 per share minus strike price of $55 per share). If the stock were to rise to $72 per share, your loss would be $1,700.

> **uncovered call**
>
> an option position involving a short call and no ownership of stock to offset the risk.

The covered call is a very strong swing trading strategy. Although it involves a short position in the call, the risks are eliminated because you own 100 shares of stock. The covered call is a valuable alternative to buying puts at a sell setup, for three reasons. First, because you *sell* the call, you receive payment of the premium when you open the covered call position. Second, when the stock's price declines, the covered call is closed with a purchase transaction, so that point drop in the stock is offset by profit in the covered call. Third, when you go short on a call, it does not matter if a lot of time value is involved. The higher the time value, the greater the premium you receive and the higher the prospects that you will make a profit. Remember, 75 percent of all options expire worthless. This is a disadvantage for the buyer, but a significant advantage for the seller. As a swing trader, you can also afford to leave a covered call open as long as you wish, because time works to your advantage.

> **naked call**
>
> alternative name for an uncovered call.

If you check Figure 9.2 once more, you can see that at notes 2 and 4, selling a covered call would produce the same profits you realize by

---

Key Point

Don't overlook the fact that when you *sell* an option, you keep the premium, even if it is exercised. For that reason, covered calls are not only conservative—they can also be profitable.

---

buying puts. You can sell one option for every 100 shares of stock that you own. The only point to remember is that you need to ensure a profit in the event the call is exercised. This means the strike price for the short call should be higher than your basis in the stock.

Because you keep the call premium paid when you open the short position, the actual net basis in stock is reduced. For example, if you sell a 55 call and receive a premium of 3 ($300), that premium is yours to keep if and when the call is exercised. So if you purchased stock at $54 per share, your profit upon exercise of the covered call would be $400 before brokerage fees:

Option premium for covered call	$300
Profit on stock	$100
Total profit	$400

The larger the gap between your original purchase price of stock and the strike price of the covered call, the greater the potential profit upon exercise. In the preceding example, the capital gain on the stock was only $100. But if the stock had been purchased at $44 per share, the profit on a 55 call upon exercise would have been:

Option premium for covered call	$300
Profit on stock	$1,100
Total profit	$1,400

The annualized return on these kinds of transactions can be in the double digits. For example, a $1,400 profit on a covered call could be quite significant on a percentage basis. If you consider the cost of $55 per share, discounted by three points in the stock, the net basis in the transaction was $5,200. A $1,400 profit is 27 percent. However, if the entire

> ### Key Point
>
> Double-digit returns with covered calls are not only possible, but probable as well. As a device for the sell setup, they are more profitable than buying puts and safer than shorting stock.

transaction took only three months, that would be an annualized 104 percent profit. There is absolutely no guarantee that you can consistently make a 100 percent profit on swing trading and covered call writing. However, this example is reasonable and such returns can and do occur using covered calls.

As part of a swing trading strategy, covered calls are interesting because they are exceptionally conservative; they produce a cash inflow instead of an outlay with long puts; and they also offset the basic swing trading risks in responding to a sell setup.

Advanced Strategies: Short Options for Swing Trading

The world of options provides a broad range of conservative and speculative strategies. You can swing trade in various configurations on both the long and the short side. While the primary emphasis here has been to *reduce* risks, you can also take much higher than average risks with options if you want. The reduction of risk is achieved by using long puts in place of shorting stock at sell setups. However, other risk considerations should be kept in mind as well. These include:

1. *Discounted stock basis with covered calls.* The actual net cost of stock is reduced when you write covered calls. Thus, as a swing trading strategy, the covered call provides you with immediate income *and* lower market risk in the stock itself.

2. *Reduced capital exposure with long calls and puts.* You can achieve the same profit from point movement with options that you get in buying stocks. But the amount of capital you put at risk is much lower.

Key Point

Diversification is one of the great advantages in using options for swing trading, in four ways: expansion of stocks for swing trading, the use of multiple option contracts, less capital at risk, and the combined use of calls (long as well as short) and puts.

---

3. *Reduced losses when false signals occur.* While options expire and become worthless upon expiration date, the typical swing trade lasts from two to five days; so as long as you call the majority of your setups correctly, you risk less capital. At those times when you are wrong, losses are limited to the cost of the option.

4. *Better diversification.* You can expand your swing trading with the use of options and put your available capital to better use. This is achieved in several ways. First, you can use options to swing trade on several different stocks, with each option giving you the same profit potential as 100 shares of stock. Second, you can use multiple options to expand potential profits and provide yourself with alternative strategies when trends turn into momentum moves. Third, you lower your risk of loss by limiting yourself to options rather than placing larger sums of capital into stock. And fourth, you improve diversification with a combination of long calls, long puts, and short covered calls.

combination
any option strategy involving the use of two or more options with dissimilar terms (call versus put, long versus short, strike price, or expiration date).

Advanced option strategies include many additional *combinations* of long and short positions in both calls and puts. These include the *spread* and the *straddle*. A spread is the purchase and sale of options with different strike prices, expiration dates, or both. A straddle is the purchase and sale of calls and puts with identical strike prices and expiration dates. Both of these strategies can be entered on either the long or short side.

These advanced strategies are complex and involve varying degrees of risk. They are appropriate for experienced options traders who can afford higher risk levels, and are beyond the scope of this book. For swing trading, however, these concepts offer new dimensions to the strategy and enable you to take many different and new positions that are not possible using the relatively simple purchase or sale of shares of stock. Ultimately, even the basic swing trading strategy is far less risky using long options than any other approach—with better diversification, flexibility, and leverage. Contrary to the reputation of options as high-risk instruments, if properly used they can vastly expand the swing trading universe with *lower* risks and higher profits.

The next chapter expands on this concept with a broad view of how swing trading fits within your overall portfolio, your risk profile, and your long-term investment program.

spread

the purchase and sale of options with different strike prices, expiration dates, or both.

straddle

the purchase and sale of calls and puts with identical strike prices and expiration dates.

Swing Trading in Your Investment Portfolio

Everyone struggles to identify the most appropriate methods for investing and trading. The vast majority of investors cannot afford indefinite losses. With limited capital available—and knowing that you never achieve 100 percent success—the goal becomes one of trying to move the odds, even slightly, in your favor.

Swing trading is a method designed to make this happen. Specific setups for buy and sell action help you to pick and time short-term cyclical changes in price. Selection of stocks appropriate for swing trading limits the field and also helps you to define your program in terms of risk and profit potential.

Even with the identification of strategies to out-perform the market, is it enough to act as a contrarian? Swing trading is in many respects the ultimate contrarian strategy because it calls for calm when the market mood is one of panic; for moderation when others are responding to greed; and for focus when the mood is uncertainty. Swing traders also learn to look for the right signals, requiring patience in a market where attention spans are short and fast, easy profits are often the goal.

Swing Trading Guidelines

Swing traders can profit when price moves up or down, and this is an important point worth remembering. Some additional guidelines include the following:

1. *It does not matter which direction price moves.* Swing trading is not geared toward the common attitude that prices *must* move upward. Investors tend to be optimists, and upward trends are more interesting when long positions are held. The vast majority of individual investors invest solely on the long side. This means that half of all opportunities are being ignored. While long-term market values may grow, there are numerous opportunities to profit when the market is falling as well. Swing trading doubles your profit-making opportunities. You are trading market emotions, not stocks, and that is the entire key to swing trading.

2. *Your entry point is part of a continuum, not a beginning.* The prices of stocks are continually on the move, and nothing goes in one direction indefinitely. Momentum trends are limited even when they are quite strong. A typical two- to five-day price swing is normal in the short-term scheme of things. So you need to view your trade entry point as a matter of stepping onto a moving vehicle. The starting price is *not* a starting point, merely the current point in an ever-changing series of uptrends and downtrends. As a swing trader, you use setups to time your entry on either long or short side. Only one thing is certain: That price is going to change.

Key Point

Swing traders do not try to pick stocks specifically; they identify investor mood and short-term trends, and exploit the emotional aspects of the market and of investor behavior.

> ## Key Point
>
> So many investors view price in unrealistic terms, thinking of their basis price as a starting point. If you view price as an unending struggle between buyers and sellers, your perspective will improve greatly.

3. *You will never achieve 100 percent perfect timing.* Even with the best information, some of your swing trades are going to result in losses. Whether you trade in shares of stock or options, swing trading is not a perfect system. You can only hope to improve your percentages and swing trading is effective for that purpose. If you set a goal for yourself that every trade must be profitable, you are going to be unhappy with the results. You should consider your strategy a success if you improve the number of profitably timed moves over your previous record.

4. *A series of small profits are preferable to the risk of one big loss.* Swing trading produces better than average profits, even though this may occur in small increments. But if you are able to earn consistent profits through swing trading, rather than the hit-or-miss approach so often practiced by speculators and other short-term traders, your overall percentages are going to improve. There is no need to increase the capital at risk in an effort to improve the dollar amount of profits. Once you identify an appropriate investment dollar level per trade, you can create and

> ## Key Point
>
> No system can promise to deliver 100 percent profitable outcomes or perfect timing. Swing trading is designed to *improve* your decisions, not to give you absolute certainty about outcomes.

maintain a steady flow of activity while managing risk levels as well. Remember, there is no such thing as a 100 percent system, so as a swing trader you are wise to limit each trade to a manageable level.

5. *An open-minded attitude to the use of options broadens the potential for swing trading profits.* The entire options market has a singular reputation of being too high-risk for the average investor. The truth is, options can be extremely risky or very conservative. They are the perfect vehicle for swing trading and, with a little practice, you can master the terminology as well as the trading rules. Simply using long calls in place of long stock, and long puts in place of short stock, vastly expands your use of capital with less risk than using stock; it allows you to diversify into more stocks; and you have greater flexibility using multiple option contracts. A more sophisticated strategy, covered call writing, is even more profitable *and* conservative for those investors with options trading experience.

6. *Cutting losses is a wise way to trade.* Every trader is going to experience losses due to poor timing or misread signals. Stock prices may also contradict the implied setup direction at time. There is a degree of random price change in the market, and setup signals reduce the risk but can never eliminate it completely. You can cut losses by closing positions as soon as you discover that prices are

---

Key Point

Swing traders create better-than-average small returns rather than risking an all-or-nothing outcome. This makes sense and over time produces better outcomes.

Key Point

When you study options in the context of swing trading, you discover that they actually *reduce* risks and expand your swing trading field of play.

> ### Key Point
>
> Just as a wise chess player knows when to retreat, traders also need to know when to cut their losses. If you manage risk by diversifying capital, you can better afford to cut losses; this is where options are useful.

> ### Key Point
>
> A lot of emphasis is placed on eliminating or avoiding risk. But on a practical level, risk cannot be avoided. However, it can be managed well.

not moving in the desired direction; and by using trailing stop orders to limit the amount of loss. Using long options instead of long or short stock also limits your potential loss on any single trade.

7. *All risks can be managed.* Risks can never be eliminated completely, but they can be managed. Swing trading presents a practical alternative to the traditional buy-and-hold concept of investing. In today's rapidly changing market, buy-and-hold is not always a practical way to beat market averages. More and more, traders seek methods such as swing trading to avoid long-term value decline. The use of options in place of stock purchase or sale enables you to manage risks effectively while expanding profit potential.

Short-Term Trading and Long-Term Investing

Every trader has to decide what market philosophy to adopt. Are you a buy-and-hold investor seeking stocks you can hold over many years? Or do you want to move in and out of positions in a matter of days? Some people also want to diversify and do both.

> ### Key Point
>
> As more investors trade in discount sites online and use the Internet for research, a growing belief has emerged: that long-term investing does not work as well as smart short-term trading. In truth, a combination of both works well.

The traditional stockbroker was set up as an advisor to people who wanted to build a permanent portfolio. By "permanent," this means the emphasis was invariably on buy-and-hold approaches to the market. Within that definition, some stocks have always been considered safer than others; so diversification among long-term hold stocks was the most popular method of portfolio management. Today, some people continue to subscribe to the buy-and-hold approach to investing. But a growing number of investors and traders are beginning to question whether it is possible or practical to hold onto the stock of one company for years, if not for decades.

The markets change more rapidly today than ever before. Traditional reliance on stockbrokers and financial planners is rapidly becoming obsolete. Today, those still in the business of earning commissions by making recommendations to people are becoming a threatened species. People have more information available today than ever before; this means that you no longer need to pay for advice.

The combination of rapidly changing markets and the availability of free market information has created a smarter, better informed class of investors. The brokerage business was always set up so that investors needed stockbrokers just to execute trades. Within a few years, the whole concept of paying people to give advice and place trades will be gone entirely. Why has this occurred?

The big change has been the Internet. Today you can go directly to the home page of virtually every listed company, and stock exchanges all link directly to their member pages. In addition, discount brokerage firms offer trading for a very low cost. They also provide free research to subscribers as well as low-cost or no-cost accounts.

Valuable Resource

To find home pages or financial summaries for listed companies, the easiest route is the exchanges themselves. Check the following websites to find links to member companies:

- New York Stock Exchange at *http://www.nyse.com*. Click the link labeled "Listed company directory."
- NASDAQ at *http://www.nasdaq.com*. Click the link labeled "Company financials."

Many financial services have been vastly changed in the past two decades. In the not so distant past, individuals with life insurance policies used to visit local offices of insurance companies to pay monthly (and even weekly) premiums in cash. Bond investors used to physically clip coupons and remit them to issuers for interest payments. And of course, until online investing and home computers revolutionized the entire market, you could not place orders directly but had to rely on the telephone to reach your stockbroker.

This revolution in technology has made all markets far more accessible to individual investors than ever before. Many other changes are occurring as well. The exchange-traded fund (ETF) is changing the way that people invest in mutual funds. Under the old system, you had to buy and sell shares directly with the fund's management, taking time and making the process cumbersome. You also had no control over the buy and sell decisions of a fund's management. The ETF identifies a basket of stocks in advance and does not change it, meaning you know what you

---

Key Point

Stockbrokers no longer play an essential role for most traders. With the Internet and online discount sites, it is not longer necessary to pay someone to place trades for you.

are getting in advance. This also means there is virtually no need to pay managers because no decisions need to be made. Shares of ETFs can be bought and sold like stocks on public exchanges, and many also offer options. This whole approach vastly changes mutual fund investing, which has been a primary emphasis for investors for many years.

People also used to rely on stockbrokers for basic information like annual reports or other analytical summaries. Today you can get free annual reports directly from any listed company or through links from most financial news sites or online brokers. These brokerage firms also provide members with free research that would cost a lot if subscribed to separately. For example, Schwab subscribers pay no fees but get free S&P Stock Reports, Reuters, Goldman Sachs, Argus, and Schwab ratings and analysis for listed companies. Other brokerage services offer a similar range of free and low-cost research to their members.

Before the Internet, swing trading would have been impossible to do efficiently. The time lag between investors and stockbrokers (as well as between stockbrokers and the floor of exchanges) was too great to efficiently or economically execute trades with a thin margin of profit. The full-commission cost was too great as well, and in the days before online discount brokerage services, few people outside of the exchanges themselves were able to execute any kind of short-term trading program effectively.

The more the Internet expands the possibilities for investors, the more practical it becomes to perform many varieties of short-term trading strategies. The use of options is also a practical vehicle for many of these strategies, if only because access to current prices and order execution is simple and the cost of trades is so low.

This broad availability of information has a negative side. With trading made so easy for everyone, it is also possible to trade without having a lot of experience and without being aware of the risks. One service responsible stockbrokers used to provide was to guide novice investors into appropriate investing avenues. Today, anyone with a

---

Key Point

The Internet has speeded up trading, quotations, and access to free information. It has also pointed out the value of short-term strategies like swing trading.

Valuable Resource

Free candlestick charts are available from several sites, including *http://www.candlestickchart.com.*

computer can open and fund a trading account. So it is especially important today for anyone, especially swing traders, to ensure that they know exactly what they are doing and what risks are involved. Even the availability of candlestick charts, a great advantage to swing traders, can be a problem. If you do not know how to read and interpret setup signals, it is all too easy to make mistakes. However, free candlestick charting makes swing trading a practical strategy today, whereas in the past traders had no such tools without paying for them, often at the rate of hundreds of dollars per year.

Assessing Risk and Opportunity

In the modern world of lightning-fast trading, easy access to research and charting tools, and low-cost transaction fees, swing trading makes good sense. It would not have been practical in the past, however. Today many traders are beginning to realize that they do not have to structure an investment strategy around a stockbroker, the cost of trading, or difficulty in locating research. For example, you can find an annual or quarterly report this instant for any listed company. You do not have to ask your stockbroker to request a copy and then wait for two weeks until the mail arrives.

This ultra-convenience makes it easier than ever to broaden your investment opportunities; it also expands the related risks that go with

Key Point

You can still send away for a hard copy annual report. But why should you? These documents can be downloaded, studied and printed online at a moment's notice.

any strategy. So it is just as important as ever to assess risk as part of your exploration of a strategy. This includes swing trading and, of course, the methods you employ and their risks. Some aspects of swing trading demanding risk evaluation include:

1. *The overall strategy.* How much swing trading should you do? How much capital should you place at risk and should you be long or short on every stock at the same time? Even investors who subscribe to the buy-and-hold approach know that they need to diversify and the question should be raised for swing trading as well. Even the true believer in swing trading may discover some wisdom in diversifying a portfolio by strategy, meaning that some capital may belong in long-term stocks, mutual funds, or non-stock investments.

2. *Short-term long position costs and risks.* The transaction cost of any strategy is always an issue and there are costs involved in both buying and selling. This cost has to be factored in to the strategy. Using options if far cheaper than buying and selling round lots of stock, and the use of multiple option contracts is extremely low in comparison to stock trades. Depending on your percentage of profitable trades, you should be aware of the transaction cost as part of your overall evaluation.

3. *Short selling stock.* Most people will agree that selling short is a high-risk approach to the market. Those investors not willing to take this risk have to limit their swing trading to only the buy setup, so that half of all opportunities are lost. This risk may be acceptable to some people, especially if they place a lot of faith in their setup pattern recognition. But this risk cannot be ignored.

4. *Option risks.* The options market is risky for several reasons. The terminology is strange and complex; time is always an issue; and the complexity of option valuation can deceive you. If you emphasize trading in short-term, in-the-money options with little or no time value, you can minimize the risk. If you buy puts instead of shorting stock, you eliminate the short sale risk. However, "experience risk" is also a factor with options. You need to understand the market thoroughly before executing actual trades.

5. *Diversification risks.* All investors and traders need to understand the many forms of diversification, and to identify the degree they require in their own portfolio. For example, you can diversify in the stocks you use for swing trading, the use of many different sectors within the market, and even in combinations of buy setups and sell setups. However, also be aware of the potential for diversification between swing trading and other strategies, such as long-term buy-and-hold, option speculation, covered call writing against long stocks in your portfolio, and the use of exchange-traded funds.

The comparison between opportunity and risk cannot be undertaken separately. It is a common mistake. Some people like to focus on the profit potential of a particular strategy but forget to also consider the directly corresponding risk. The two cannot be looked at as different aspects of an investment decision; they are two aspects of the same attribute. The profit potential and risk to any strategy are inseparable. This is a fact worth remembering, because it is all too easy to focus only on the optimistic side of things.

Risk may also be viewed as a means for checking yourself. On paper, many strategies appear both exciting and profitable. It is easy to convince yourself that you have a "sure thing." In swing trading, you may observe the consistency of past price behavior follow a narrow range day or engulfing line and become convinced that these setups always work. However, that is not the case. They work most of the time, but it remains quite possible that stock price will defy the signals and move in the "wrong" direction. This is defined as a direction that produces a loss instead of a profit—a point to always keep in mind.

Diversification by Risk Profile

Of the many varieties of diversification, one of the most important is based on your personal risk profile. Any discussion of risk is based on a broad assumption that each individual possesses a singular, specific risk level and all investments in the portfolio have to conform to that profile. In practice, this is rarely true. Most people are more complex than that and cannot be defined so narrowly.

For example, you may assume a highly conservative stance regarding your family's home and savings accounts, but a higher risk stance for your stock portfolio. Your home is insured and maintained, and you might even resist the temptation to mortgage it excessively, being aware of cash flow and equity versus debt levels. Your savings account may yield relatively low rates but it is in an insured account. These are very conservative forms of investment.

Your stock portfolio may be set up with a somewhat more aggressive stance. You might be willing to take some degree of risk hoping to beat market averages. You may buy some stocks for long-term hold, put some funds into mutual funds, and use the remainder of your funds in options or speculation in stocks. This is where swing trading comes into play; you might divide your overall portfolio into many different segments and identify varying levels of risk appropriate to each. Your "safety net" investments (home and savings) should be very conservative; your stock portfolio may be somewhat risky; and some portion of your equity may be devoted to swing trading, using either stock positions or long options.

As long as you define each of these segments, and control the levels of funds placed into each, you will have diversified not only by the type of investment (real estate, money market, and equity) but also by risk profile. This strategy of managing your portfolio, called *asset allocation*, is not always described in terms of personal risk. It is more commonly

---

Key Point

You do not have to accept a single definition of "appropriate" risks and then invest only in products meeting that definition. You are likely to find that you can involve yourself with many different risk levels.

discussed in terms of diversifying by markets. It is also possible to diversify among markets while still conforming to a narrowly defined risk level. The preceding example demonstrates how asset allocation can be used to enrich your own risk diversification as well.

asset allocation
a method of managing a portfolio by dividing funds among several different markets; an advanced technique for diversifying a portfolio.

Asset allocation is most often described in terms of percentages. And while every investor is different, some market observers have attempted to assign a universal percentage recommendation based on current economic conditions. In this variation, the assumption is that every investor should react in the same way to changing economic conditions. It makes more sense, however, to view asset allocation as a risk-based form of variation within a portfolio. It might not be appropriate, for example, to devote all of your investment assets to swing trading. For example, you may have diversified your portfolio for college education, retirement, and current income. The ultimate goals of each of these segments to your portfolio dictate the appropriate levels of risk; with this in mind, swing trading may be appropriate but should be determined by the conservatism of the investment goal itself.

No one individual can be accurately described as being a "conservative" investor or a "speculator" in all instances. The actual determination of the products and risks you select is going to be based on many factors, including:

1. *Your understanding of a specific market.* If you thoroughly understand a market you are going to be more likely to take part in it. Some markets frighten people away because they are complex; options, for example, are not as high-risk as they are perceived by many people. But the definitions and unique characteristics of

---

Key Point

Contrary to what the financial planning industry has claimed for years, "risk" is not simply unique to a person or family. It should vary based on the goals within the portfolio, and that often means that you will have several different appropriate risk levels.

options make them especially troubling to anyone not familiar with how they work. The more you understand how a market works, the better suited you are to identifying ways that you can make use of the products.

2. *Preferred risk levels and ability to place funds at risk.* People do tend to invest money in specific ways. Some are highly conservative and, as a general rule, will be willing to accept lower than average returns to avoid risk. Others are more likely to speculate, seeking exceptionally high returns in exchange for much greater risks. Most people find themselves somewhere between these extremes.

3. *Current income and asset levels.* Your risk profile changes as your income increases and as your overall net worth grows or shrinks. So a new career or job, divorce, or other significant economic changes in your life are also going to directly affect your risk profile. It is important to be aware of these changes and to be able to change your portfolio to match your actual situation.

4. *Apprehension level concerning the economic future.* As perceptions about economic and political conditions change, so will your risk profile. Even if you are not affected by changing interest rates or oil prices, the market as a whole reacts to these matters, and that means your ability to profit in a specific market or strategy are affected as well.

A Place for Swing Trading

Even in the most conservative portfolio, swing trading can play a role. For example, every investor focusing on a buy-and-hold strategy needs to decide how to deal with sudden price changes, both upward and downward. Swing trading solves this dilemma without violating the long-term goal.

Key Point

Swing trading does not have to be used only as an alternative to buy-and-hold. It can also provide better management of a permanent portfolio, in several ways.

In the typical scenario, you buy stock with the idea that you are going to keep shares indefinitely. The plan includes purchasing more shares if and when you can afford it, reinvesting dividends, and seeking stocks with similar attributes to expand the portfolio. And then one of three things occurs and the whole plan falls apart. These events are:

1. *The stock price rises.* When the price rises, even the most conservative investor is tempted to take profits; and many do just that. So now you have a different problem: You have gotten your profits but you now need to reinvest funds, and chances are all of the stocks you have been following are up at the same time.

   The danger in profit-taking is damaging to your long-term goals because it results in selling the strongest stocks. As a result, you are likely to end up with a portfolio full of stocks that have not risen in price or that have fallen in price. The goal of accumulating profits has not occurred.

2. *The stock price falls.* Another problem occurs when the price falls. It is a common reaction to want to cut losses and sell the stock. So again, the long-term plan falls apart and is replaced with an immediate gut reaction. Investors who consider themselves oriented toward long-term hold strategies should carefully pick stocks and then keep them. But in the emotional turmoil of the day-to-day market, that advice is not as easy to follow.

3. *Bad news or rumor brings doubt into the equation.* The market thrives on rumors. They are continually going around and many prove to not be true. Whether news is obtained from wire services or chat rooms, a lot of information is of questionable value. Even the reliable news leads to an over-reaction. For example, a company whose profits exceed previous years may see its stock go down because the outcome is one cent lower than analysts' predictions. The unending swell of news, both true and false, and the tendency for investors to rely so heavily on unreliable sources, leads to great chaos.

The usual market reaction to these events is greed, fear and uncertainty. These are the three emotions that drive the market and define the opportunities swing traders are able to exploit. Because the price trends are likely to evolve over a two- to five-day period, swing trading matches

---

Key Point

Remember, the market is dominated by three emotions: greed, fear and uncertainty. You can use swing trading to respond to those emotions rather than falling into the common trap of over-reacting.

---

these common cyclical price movements. The wise swing trader may also be a long-term investor, but recognizing the role of price swings is important, if only to remind long-term investors that they should not react too emotionally to short-term changes. To do so contradicts the advantage to swing trading.

Long-term investors are tempted to take profits when prices rise, or to cut losses when prices fall. It makes more sense to stay with the long-term plan and leave the stock in place; and to employ swing trading contrary to the usual tendencies based on emotion. When prices rise unexpectedly, look for a sell setup and use long puts or covered calls to provide downside protection (and, through swing trading, to take profits without selling stock). When prices fall, remain calm and look for buy setups, and then use long calls in anticipation of an offsetting uptrend.

The point to be made here is that the long-term approach involving a buy-and-hold strategy does not necessarily contradict how swing trading works. In many respects, using swing trading to augment a long-term investment strategy is both wise and profitable. It helps avoid the temptation to take profits or to sell to cut losses. It protects positions and creates short-term income while leaving equity positions in place. When you employ covered calls at sell setups, you create immediate income from the sold option, which is a form of profit-taking—especially if the stock's price does retreat. You will be able to close the call at a profit, offsetting a reduced stock price. This also protects your equity in the long stock position.

You may also employ variations to swing trading. The day trader has the goal of moving in and out of positions within a single trading day, often in distrust of the gap between trading cycles and at times as a way to get around margin requirements. However, day traders executing high volume may be required to deposit $25,000 as pattern day traders, so the system does not get around the margin rules effectively.

> ## Key Point
>
> Swing traders are by definition focused on a two- to five-day window. However, this can be varied depending on personal preferences and circumstances.

Swing trading can also be modified to respond to specific changes between one day's closing price and the next day's opening. Price gaps and reversals often signal a change in the established trend—and they may signal swing traders to reexamine their positions and, perhaps, execute a trade responding to the price trend. So an *intraday trader* is an individual who is acting as a day trader or swing trader but paying extra attention to day-to-day price changes, notably gaps.

intraday trader

a swing trader or day trader who may modify positions based on price gaps or reversals occurring from one trading day to the next.

Another variation on swing trading involves an accelerated period. Instead of observing a two- to five-day trend and tracking daily charts, the *micro trader* watches 5-minute and 15-minute charts as well as 20-period and 200-period moving averages. A moving average is usually described in terms of *days*, but micro traders involve periods of time increments. So a 20-period moving average consists of 20 sequential five-minute periods; and a 200-period moving average would involve 200 sequential five-minute periods.

micro trader

a trader who looks for trading setup patterns within a single day often involving the study of five-minute and 15-minute price periods.

The micro trader also pays attention to specific reversal signals occurring at exact trading times during the day. These traders observe a tendency for the typical day to exhibit a morning and afternoon trend in the same direction, with a middle period relatively flat and with low volume. These trends signal how and when to look for buy or sell setup signals in greatly accelerated time. Rather than waiting up to five days, the micro trader may make trades within five five-minute increments.

You may discover your own variations on swing trading as you study and practice the many techniques available. The valuable free online tools that make swing trading both practical and affordable can also

---

Key Point

Everything has changed in the market over the past two or three decades—including the reality that investors are either smarter or *should* be smarter through access to so many market tools.

---

serve as educational tools as you master the candlestick chart, moving averages, and other features. In the past, swing trading was not practical because the average investor had no direct access to the markets. Today, your access is fast and much better than access for the stockbroker of the past. Investor knowledge is also far more sophisticated today than ever before.

The exceptional opportunities for swing trading have made the markets not only accessible, but easier to interpret. Only a few short decades ago, insiders held market facts close to the vest and promoted an aura of mystery, and most people trusted in the system. Today, you—the individual investor—*are* the system, and now you are able to create and control your own profits.

Glossary

Regulation T a Federal Reserve Board rule establishing and governing rules for margin borrowing in brokerage accounts.

against the box a strategy for going short when the trader owns shares. The short sale is made against the shares in the portfolio rather than borrowed from another investor.

ascending channel a channel with a rising trading range over time. Short-term swings in price occur, but the longer-term price trend is upward.

asset allocation a method of managing a portfolio by dividing funds among several different markets; an advanced technique for diversifying a portfolio.

at the money a situation where an option's strike price is identical to the stock's current market value.

bearish engulfing line a candlestick engulfing line—one extending above and below the previous trading day's main body—with a black main body.

black candlestick a candlestick with a black real body showing that the stock moved down on the day.

blocks large trades of stock executed by institutional investors in most cases, usually defined as 10,000 or more shares or stock with current value of $200,000 or more.

breakaway gap a gap involving price movement into new territory beyond the established trading range.

breakout a pattern in which price moves above resistance or below support and establishes a new trend and, eventually, a new trading range.

broadening formations chart patterns showing widening trading range for a stock, developing over time and providing specific signals for swing traders.

broker call rate the rate many brokers charge clients for borrowing funds on margin; the rate a firm charges is normally found on the brokerage website.

bullish engulfing line a candlestick engulfing line—one extending above and below the previous trading day's main body—with a white main body.

buy stop a type of order that generates an automate buy if and when the stock moves to or above a specified price.

buy to close an order that closes a short investment, which involves buying the security and number of shares to cancel out the open position.

buy to open   the first order in a long position, which instructs the broker to purchase the indicated security and number of shares or contracts.

buying power   the margin allowance a brokerage firm provides to a pattern day trader, which is a multiple of available equity balance in the portfolio.

call   an option granting its owner the right (but not the requirement) to buy 100 shares of a specific stock at a fixed price per share.

candlestick   a chart formation showing each day's trading range; high and low price; opening and closing price; and the direction the price moved for the day. A white (or clear) candlestick reveals that the price closed higher than its open; and a black candlestick reflects a lower close for the day.

capitalization   the total funding of an operation, include equity (stock) and debt (bonds and long-term loans).

cash flow   the cash available from operations to pay current and long-term expenses and liabilities; fund business expansion; and pay dividends.

channel   the overall direction of a stock's price movement; the trend, which may be flat, upward, or downward over many months.

chartists   technical analysts who rely primarily on recognition of specific price patterns and short-term trends to predict and anticipate the next price direction in a stock's price.

combination   any option strategy involving the use of two or more options with dissimilar terms (call versus put, long versus short, strike price, or expiration date).

common doji   another name for the doji, distinguished from other doji variations.

common gap   another term for the gap, which distinguishes it from other forms of exceptional gap chart patterns.

concealing baby swallow   a bullish candlestick pattern consisting of a series of four black real bodies in a declining trend, anticipating a reversal in coming trades.

confirmation   a signals that provides additional indication to another signal, that reinforces the indicated timing of a buy or sell move.

consolidation   a time when price is not moving upward or downward, but remaining within a narrow trading range; a market dominated by uncertainty.

contingent liability   a liability that might or might not materialize, and whose dollar value may not be known. Typically, outstanding lawsuits that have not been settled or decided are the best-known form of such contingencies.

contingent order   any order to buy or sell based on specific price levels being reached or passed. This type of order is used to protect existing profits or to avoid large losses in the event of sudden price movement.

core earnings   the earnings as reported by a company, adjusted to remove all reported earnings that are not part of a corporation's "core" business, including nonrecurring revenues and net earnings.

correction   the description of a market in which prices are falling, when the emotion of fear dominates the market.

cover   a short seller's action in buying to close, in which the exposed short position is covered through cancellation.

covered call   an option strategy in which a call is sold, but the seller also owns 100 shares of the stock. In the event the call is exercised, the 100 shares are used to satisfy the call.

current yield   the percentage paid in dividends, calculating by dividing declared dividends by current price of the stock.

day order   a type of order placed with a broker specifying that if it is not executed by the end of the trading day, it automatically expires.

day trade call   a requirement that investors deposit funds to satisfy pattern day trading deposit requirements based on the volume of trades (four or more trades in the same security within five trading days).

day trader   an individual who executes trades within a single day or over the shortest possible time, often moving in and out of positions within a matter of hours and employing a high volume of trading activity.

debt ratio   the portion of capitalization represented by debt; to compute, divide long-term liabilities by total capitalization, expressing the result as a percentage.

deliberation   a bearish candlestick appearing within at uptrend, involving three consecutive white real bodies closing higher than the previous day, with the final day opening with a gap above the previous close.

descending channel   a trading range moving downward in price over a period of months.

diversification   one of several methods of spreading risk, involving exposure to different products, markets, or stocks. For corporations, diversification also refers to investment in dissimilar lines of business.

dividend yield   the profit earned from dividends paid by corporations, expressed as a percentage of the current price. For calculation purposes, the percentage should always be based on stock purchase price rather than current price.

do not reduce (DNR)   instructions attached to an order to keep a limit price even when cash dividends occur. Without the DNR, the limit price is automatically reduced for dividends earned.

doji   a candlestick with little or no real body, shaped like a cross. This demonstrates very little change between opening and closing prices, with trading occurring above and below those levels.

double bottom   a price pattern testing support with a price increase in between. Because support holds up against this two-part test, the double bottom anticipates a subsequent increase in the price level.

double top   a price pattern in which resistance is tested twice with a pullback in between. As long as resistance holds up, price is expected to decline after the double top.

Dow Theory   a major technical school of thought, a belief that overall market movement is predictable based on primary and secondary trends and confirming signals. The Dow Theory states that short-term trends are not reliable for predicting long-term price changes.

downtrend   a movement in a stock's price to the downside; for swing traders, a downtrend is defined as three or more consecutive days in which the closing price was lower than the opening price.

dragonfly doji   a candlestick with little or no distance between opening and closing prices, but a trading range below that level for the day.

efficient market hypothesis   the theory that pricing of stocks reflects all information currently known by investors at any given time, resulting in the conclusion that all stock prices are fair and reasonable.

engulfing line   a candlestick pattern in which the main body of a trading day extends higher *and* lower than the main body of the previous trading day.

equity investment   a form of ownership in a corporation, the best-known form of which is stock.

ex-dividend   the date of ownership for the purpose of paying dividends. The owner of shares on the specified date is entitled to the dividend, even if shares are sold after that date but before dividend payment date (when shares are said to be trading ex-dividend). The ex-date is the dividing point.

exhaustion gap   a type of gap in the direction of an extended price movement, signaling that the current trend is about to end and prices will level out or begin moving in the opposite direction.

expiration   the deadline for an option and the date on which it loses all of its value.

extrinsic value   the value of an option not counting any intrinsic value; the time value premium, given this alternate name to consider the non-time elements of volatility within the stock, and of proximity between stock's current market value and the option's strike price.

fill or kill (FOK)   a condition attached to a limit order instructing your broker to complete the order immediately or, if that is not possible, to cancel the order right away.

financial statement   a report published by a corporation reporting activity over a period of time, such as a full year (the operating statement) or balances of asset, liability and net worth accounts at the end of a period (the balance sheet).

flat channel   a channel whose trading range remains the same over time, with neither rising or falling price trend exhibited for a period of months.

fundamental analysis   the valuation of stocks based on a company's financial strength, earnings, and trends, including assessment of working capital, equity and debt capitalization, and operating results.

fundamental volatility   the degree of consistency or change in reported revenues and earnings from one year to the next.

gap   a price pattern in which one day's opening price is higher than the previous day's highest price or lower than the previous day's lowest price.

go short   a transaction beginning with a sell order, later to close with an offsetting buy order.

good 'til canceled (GTC)   a condition attached to an order to leave it open indefinitely until it can be filled on the terms the investor requires; brokerage firms will let such orders expire after a specified time period.

gravestone doji   a candlestick with little or no space between opening and closing price, but a trading range above those levels for the day.

hammer   a candlestick pattern occurring at the end of a downtrend. It consists of a long lower shadow and a small real body, and signals a reversal and the start of an uptrend.

hangman   a candlestick pattern occurring at the end of an uptrend. It consists of a long lower shadow and a small real body and signals a reversal and the start of a downtrend.

head-and-shoulders bottom   the inverse of a top, consisting of a head testing support with two shorter shoulders before and after, creating a letter w shape. The pattern anticipates a price increase.

head-and-shoulders bottom   the inverse of a top, consisting of a head testing support with two shorter shoulders before and after, creating a letter W shape. The pattern anticipates a price increase.

head-and-shoulders top   a price pattern with three peaks, the middle one higher than the first and third. This letter m shape pattern tests resistance and anticipates a price decline to follow.

hedge   a position taken in a security to offset or eliminate risks in another position. For example, going short may be used as a way to protect paper profits in long positions.

house requirement   the maintenance requirement set by brokerage firms, which is equal to or greater than the minimum 25 percent required under NASD and NYSE rules.

immediate or cancel   a condition allowing a broker to fill part of an order if the entire order cannot be completed; and on the stipulation that this be done right away and any remaining portions canceled.

in the money   condition of an option when the strike price of a call is lower than current stock price, or when the strike price of a put is higher than the current stock price.

initial margin   a limit on the level of borrowing investors are allowed by the Federal Reserve Board's Regulation T. It specifies that you can only borrow up to 50 percent of a security's purchase price.

institutional investors   large investors such as mutual funds, insurance companies or pension plans, holding diversified portfolios of stock and trading in blocks rather than only a few hundred shares. Institutional investors account for most of the market's treading volume.

internal diversification   a form of corporate diversification of capital into dissimilar product or service lines of business.

intraday trader   a swing trader or day trader who may modify positions based on price gaps or reversals occurring from one trading day to the next.

intrinsic value   the premium value of an option equal to the number of points it is in the money (current market value higher than a call's strike price or lower than a put's strike price).

leverage   an investing strategy using borrowed funds to broaden a portfolio beyond available cash resources.

limit order   a type of order specifying execution of a buy at or below a specified price, or of a sell order at or above a specified price.

long position   ownership of stock and other securities, entered by execution or trades in the sequence buy-hold-sell.

long-legged doji   a candlestick with little or no distance between opening and closing prices but exceptionally broad trading range above and below.

long-term hold   description of a strategy for portfolio management, involving selection of stocks with the intention of holding shares for many years in order to build a secure base for long-term growth.

long-term liabilities   all liabilities due and payable beyond the next 12 months (the current portion), including notes, contracts and bonds.

lower shadow   in a candlestick, the trading range between the day's low price and the bottom of the real body (opening or closing price).

maintenance requirement   the percentage of current market value of securities that must be kept in a portfolio at all times. Minimum federal requirement is 25 percent, but some brokerage firms require higher maintenance levels.

margin call   a demand from a brokerage firm for additional deposits by investors whose maintenance requirement has not been met due to portfolio losses. If the margin call is not met, the brokerage firm will sell securities from the account.

margin   investing using funds borrowed from a brokerage firm, with securities in an account used as collateral.

market order   an order to buy or sell as quickly as possible and at the best available price. Execution is guaranteed, but price is not.

market risk   the risk that a stock's value will fall rather than rise (or rise after an investor sells). Market risk can be compared and judged based on fundamental trends and technical price history.

marubozu   a candlestick with a real body but no upper or lower shadow; a day whose trading range is confined within opening and closing prices.

micro trader   a trader who looks for trading setup patterns within a single day often involving the study of five-minute and 15-minute price periods.

minimum margin   the deposit requirement to set up a margin account, which is the lesser of $2,000 or 100 percent of the security's purchase price.

momentum   in technical analysis, the rate and speed of changes in price and trading range, believed to be a determining factor in how soon a trading pattern is likely to adjust.

moving average   a statistical method of showing a trend that is representative of changes without short-term volatility. The average is computed by adding up the fields in the period, and then dividing by the number of trading days.

multiple   the P/E of a stock, arrived at by dividing price per share by earnings per share. The multiple is expressed as a single numerical value.

naked call   alternative name for an uncovered call.

narrow range day   a day in which the high-to-low price of a day is much smaller than the typical day, and when it occurs after three or more established trend day patterns.

neckline   the price area in between the price extremes of the head and shoulders pattern.

new high   the highest price a stock has reached during the past 52 weeks.

new low   the lowest price a stock has reached during the past 52 weeks.

OHLC chart   a type of stock chart summarizing the open, high, low, and close for a day using a single vertical line and two horizontal tabs The top of the vertical line is the line and the bottom is the low; the left tab is the day's opening price and the right tab is the day's closing price.

operating statement   a financial statement summarizing all activity—revenue, costs and expenses, and profits—for a specified period of time, most often a full year or a fiscal quarter.

option   an intangible contract granting its owner specific rights to either buy or sell 100 shares of a specific stock, on or before a specific date, for a specific price per share.

or better   in a limit order, the terms for completion of a transaction. In a buy order, execution is to occur when a specified price or lower has been reached; and with a sell order, execution is to occur when a specified price or higher has been reached.

out of the money   condition of an option when the strike price of a call is higher than the current stock price, or when the strike price of a put is lower than the current stock price.

P/E ratio   a test comparing technical and fundamental information. The price per share is divided by earnings per share to arrive at the multiple. The P/E is an effective way to compare stocks and to limit stock selection. The result of dividing price per share by earnings per share is expressed as a single numerical value, known as the multiple.

paper profits   the profits in existing stock positions, which become realized profits only if and when those positions are closed.

parallel price channels   the top and bottom edges of a trading range when price levels are evolving to the upside or downside, as opposed to a range in which prices remain stable within the range.

pattern day trader   as defined by the SEC, any trader who buys or sells a single stock four or more times within five days; a pattern day trader must maintain no less than $25,000 account equity before a high volume of trading is permitted.

point-and-figure chart   a stock chart reflecting rising prices with columns of Xs extending from high to low price; and columns of stack's Xs. This chart does not distinguish trading days, only trends.

power spike   a price spike above or below trading range accompanied by unusually high volume or other price patterns and signaling a change in the chart pattern.

premium   the value or cost of an option, which varies according to the distance between strike price and current market value; and the time remaining until expiration.

price range   the overall range of a stock's price within a single day, from highest price attained down to lowest price, and distinct from opening and closing prices.

pump and dump   a strategy to buy shares and then spread rumors intended to drive up prices, after which shares are sold at a profit.

put   an option granting its owner the right (but not the requirement) to sell 100 shares of a specific stock at a fixed price per share.

rally   a period when prices are rising, also known as a condition where greed dominates the market.

random walk theory   a belief that all pricing of stocks is random, and that at any time there is a 50/50 chance that a stock's price will either rise or fall. This theory discounts the value of fundamental analysis and assumes that stock pricing is a battle between buyers and sellers for purely technical reasons.

reaction swings   short-term changes in price trend resulting from the reaction of buyers to sellers and vice versa.

real body   in a candlestick chart, the rectangular central part. A white real body shows the stock moved up from opening to closing price. A black real body shows the stock moved down from opening to closing price.

resistance   the highest price within a trading range, representing the top price that buyers are willing to pay for the stock under current conditions.

retail investor   an individual, in comparison to an institutional investor. The retail investor traditionally paid higher fees to trade, which explains the name. Today, any individual—even one paying low fees with a discount brokerage—is defined as a retail investor.

reversal signal   any chart pattern or trend implying that the current price direction is about to stop and begin moving in the opposite direction.

risk tolerance   the level of risk an individual is able and willing to assume. Risk and potential profit are directly related and cannot be accepted, so those seeking better than average profits also need to expand their risk tolerance.

round lot   the usual trading increment for stocks, which is 100 shares.

runaway gap   a gap appearing as part of a strong and sustained price trend, reinforcing the price direction, and possibly showing up as a series of gaps one after another.

sell to close   an order that closes a long investment, which involves selling the security and number of shares to cancel out the open position.

sell to open   the first order in a short position, which instructs the broker to sell the indicated security and number of shares or contracts.

setup   a signal to act in a swing trade pattern; the setup at the top of an uptrend is a sell signal, the setup at the bottom of a downtrend is a buy signal.

shadow   in a candlestick, the area above and below the real body; the trading range above and below the opening and closing prices.

shaven bottom   a candlestick with no lower shadow and a black real body; this appears on a day when the stock fell and closed at its low of the day.

shaven head   a candlestick with no upper shadow and a white real body. This appears on a day when the stock rise and closed at its high of the day.

short and distort   a short position variation of the pump and dump strategy; speculators open short positions and then spread rumors intended to frighten investors into selling their stock to drive prices down. After the price falls, short positions are covered at a profit.

short interest   a market indicator, reporting the number of shares of a specific stock that are sold short and open, and often used by investors to time market decisions.

short position   the sale of stock and other securities that is eventually closed with a purchase transaction. In a short position, the sequence of events is sell-hold-buy.

speculators   individuals willing to take greater than average risks in exchange for the opportunity for higher than average profits.

spike   an unusual price movement, above or below established trading range, and often followed by a return to that range.

spinning top   a candlestick with a large upper shadow and a small lower shadow and with a small real body that is either white or black.

spread   the point difference between high and low prices within a trading range; the larger the spread, the greater the price volatility.

spread   the purchase and sale of options with different strike prices, expiration dates, or both.

stop orders   types of orders that generate execution once a stop price has been met or passed (below for buy orders and above for sell orders). Once the stop price has been met or passed, the trade is executed.

straddle   the purchase and sale of calls and puts with identical strike prices and expiration dates.

strike price   the fixed buy or sell price of stock specified in the option contract.

supply and demand   the forces determining whether prices rise or fall. Increases in demand create upward price pressure, and increases in supply create downward price pressure; supply and demand are the causes of all stock price changes.

support   the lowest price within a trading range, representing the lowest price at which sellers will release their stock under current conditions.

swing trading   a strategy that involves two- to five-day market cycles and identifies high and low points in short-term cycles; and flags key points for moving in and out of stock positions based on specific chart pattern signals.

technical analysis   the study of stock price and volume trends, charts, and trading patterns, for the purpose of anticipating short-term price movement to time trades.

three black crows   a bearish candlestick pattern consisting of three or more black real body days in a downtrend.

three white soldiers   a bullish candlestick occurring at the end of a downtrend, consisting of three or more consecutive white real bodies closing higher on each day.

time value   the portion of an option's premium excluding any intrinsic value.

trading range   the normal trading area extending from the highest to the lowest typical price. Stocks tend to trade within a specific range. The broader the range, the greater the volatility and thus the greater the market risk.

trailing stop   a trading order that sets a percentage below current price. If and when the stock falls to that price or below, a sale is generated automatically.

triangle   a price pattern in which the trading range narrows, a sign of uncertainty about the stock's price movement and a precursor of a coming upward or downward trend.

uncovered call   an option position involving a short call and no ownership of stock to offset the risk.

underlying stock   the stock on which options are written and bought or sold.

upper shadow   in a candlestick, the trading range between the day's high price and the top of the real body (opening or closing price).

uptick rule   a Securities and Exchange Commission (SEC) rule limiting short selling activity to prevent price manipulation; stock can be sold short only when the latest trade was higher than the trade preceding it.

uptrend   a movement in a stock's price to the upside; for swing traders, an uptrend is defined as three or more consecutive days in which the closing price was higher than the opening price.

volatility   the degree of movement in a stock's price, and the number of points of movement from day to day. The greater the price swing, the higher a stock's volatility. Most investors define market risk in terms of price volatility.

white candlestick   a candlestick with a white or clear real body indicating that the stock moved up on the day.

zero-plus tick   price movement of a stock when price rises at least in its minimum increment in the latest trade.

Index

A

Accutrade, 98
against the box, 132
Alberto-Culver, 77–78
Altria Corporation, 74, 108,
    122–123, 158
Amazon.com, 20
American Express, 98
Anheuser-Busch, 170–171
Apple Computer, 158
Argus, 186
ascending channel, 74
asset allocation, 190–191
at the money, 140, 141

B

Bank One OneInvest, 98
Bank of America, 158
black candlestick, 47
Blockbuster, 70–71
blocks, 29
Bloomberg, 63
breakaway gap, 34–35
breakouts, 31–34
broker call rate, 98–99
brokerage rules, 95–99
BrownCo, 98
buy stop, 85
buy to open or close, 125–126
buying power, 101

C

calls, 138
candlestick
  black, 47
  broadening formations, 39
  concealing baby swallow, 59–60
  defined, 45
  deliberation, 61–62
  doji, 49–51
  double top and bottom, 35–36
  dragonfly doji, 49–51
  engulfing line, 55–58, 66, 69-70, 84
  gravestone doji, 49–51
  hammer, 52
  hangman, 52–53
  head-and-shoulders patterns, 37–38
  marubozu, 59
  origins, 17
  patterns, 51–58
  real body, 46
  revelations, 46–51
  reverse signal, 52
  shadow, 46–48
  shaven head and bottom, 48–49
  similarities, 59–63
  sources, 63–64
  spinning top, 49
  three black crows, 59–60
  three white soldiers, 61–62
  triangles, 39–40
  white, 47

Candlestickchart.com, 58, 64, 187
capitalization, 115
cash flow, 114
channel, 73
Charles Schwab Corporation, 20, 63, 73–74, 98, 186
chart
  candlestick, 17, 45–64
  chartists and use of, 18–19
  moving average, 16–17
  OHLC, 16, 17, 63
  patterns, 35–43, 51–58
  point-and-figure, 16
  watching, 15–20
chartists, 18–19
chart-watching, 15–20
Chevron, 158
Citigroup, 54, 122, 158
Cititrade, 98
CNN, 63
Coca-Cola, 120, 122
combination, 176
common gap, 33, 35
concealing baby swallow, 59–60
confirmation, 15
ConocoPhillips, 158
consolidation, 20–21
contingent liability, 109
contingent order, 91–93
contrarian investing, 4–5, 22, 179
core earnings, 107
correction, 20–21
cover, 131
current yield, 114

D

day order, 89
day trade call, 100–101
day trader, 7, 8–15
debt ratio, 116
deliberation, 61–62

descending channel, 74–75
Diebold, 167–168
dividend yield, 111, 114
dividendachievers.com, 113
do not reduce (DNR), 90
Dogs of the Dow, 113
doji, 49–51
Dow Theory, 30–31
Dow, Charles, 30–31
downtrend, 10–13
dragonfly doji, 49–51

E

Eastman Kodak, 108
eBay, 20
efficient market hypothesis, 2
engulfing line, 55–58, 66, 69–70, 84
equity investments, 136–137
E-Trade, 63, 98
exchange-traded fund (ETF), 185–186
ex-dividend, 90–91
exhaustion gap, 34–35
expiration of options, 138, 148–149, 162
extrinsic value, 146
Exxon Mobil, 158

F

Federal Express, 83–84
Federal Reserve Board, 87–88, 96–97
Fidelity, 98
fill or kill (FOK), 89
financial statement, 111
Firstrade, 98
flat channel, 73
Forbes, 63
Ford Motor Company, 57
fundamental analysis
  capitalization, 115
  contingent liability, 109

core earnings, 107
criteria, 117
debt ratio, 118
defined, 4
distinguished, 15
financial statement, 111
indicators, 110–116
long-term liabilities, 116
operating statement, 111
tests, 105
volatility, 107

G

gaps, 32–35
General Electric, 158
General Motors, 120–123, 158
go short, 125
Goldman Sachs, 158, 186
good 'til canceled (GTC), 90, 92
Google, 158
gravestone doji, 49–51

H

hammer, 52
hangman, 52–53
Harrisdirect, 98
hedge, 130
Hewlett-Packard, 158
Hormel Foods, 76
house requirement, 98

I

immediate or cancel, 89–90
in the money, 140, 141, 146–147
initial margin, 96–97
institutional investors, 29
Intel, 158
internal diversification, 108
intraday trader, 195
intrinsic value, 140, 143

J

Johnson and Johnson, 68–69,
    149–151, 154, 156
JP Morgan Chase, 158

K

Kraft Foods, 108
Krispy Kreme, 19, 20

L

leverage, 95
limit order, 88–89
long position, 92
long-term hold, 6
long-term liabilities, 116
lower shadow, 48
Lucent Technologies, 111–112

M

maintenance requirement, 97
margin call, 98
margin, 95
market order, 88
market risk, 23–24
marubozu, 59
Merck, 122
Mergent Corporation, 113
micro trader, 195
Microsoft, 56, 71–72, 158
minimum margin, 96
momentum, 26
moving average, 16–17
MSN Money, 63
multiple, 115

N

naked call, 173
narrow range day, 14, 70
NASDAQ, 185

National Association of Securities
  Dealers (NASD)
  brokerage rules, 87–88
  day trading rules, 99
  margin accounts, 96
  pump and dump rules, 133
  Rule 2520, 95, 99
new high and low prices, 81–82
New York Stock Exchange (NYSE),
  95, 99, 185
Newmont Mining, 158
Newton's Third Law, 65–66

O

OHLC chart, 16, 17
operating statement, 111
options
  at the money, 139–140, 141
  call, 138
  combination, 176
  consequences and risks, 160–164,
    188
  covered calls, 172–175
  defined, 135
  exotic reputation, 162
  expiration, 138, 148–149, 162
  extrinsic value, 146
  in the money, 140, 141,
    146–147
  incremental additions, 171
  intrinsic value, 140, 143
  multiple contracts, 167–172
  naked call, 173
  out of the money, 140, 141
  premium, 139
  put, 138
  short, 175–177
  spread, 176–177
  stock selection for, 164–167
  straddle, 176–177
  strike price, 138

time value, 140, 142, 143–146
trading examples, 149–156
uncovered call, 173
underlying stock and, 138
or better, 89
out of the money, 140, 141

P

P/E ratio, 114–115
paper profits, 92–93
parallel price channels, 25–26
pattern day trader, 7, 99–100
Pepsi Cola, 68–69
Pfizer, 122–123, 158
Phillip Morris, 108
point-and-figure chart, 16
Polaroid, 108
power spike, 75
premium of options, 139
price range, 11
price spikes, 75–78
price volatility, 107, 119–123
primary emotions of the market,
  20–22
Proctor & Gamble, 149–151,
  153, 156
pump and dump, 133
puts, 138

R

rally, 20–21
random walk theory, 2–3
reaction swing
  actions, 67–65
  ascending channel, 74
  channels, 73
  defined, 65
  descending channel, 74–75
  end of, 82–85
  flat channel, 73

management of, 78–82
price and volume spikes, 75–78
trading cycles, 67–68
real body, 46
Regulation T, 97, 99, 101
retail investors, 29–30
Reuters, 186
reverse signal, 52
risk tolerance, 94–95, 103
round lot, 137
runaway gap, 34–35

S

S&P Stock Reports, 186
Scott Trade, 63, 99
sector leaders, 118
Securities and Exchange Commission
    (SEC)
  day trading rules of, 7, 99
  Krispy Kreme and, 19–20
  margin regulations, 96–97
  oversight, 87
  pump and dump rules, 133
  website, 88
sell to open or close, 125–126
setup, 14
shadow area, 46–47
shaven head and bottom, 48–49
Sherwin-Williams,
    149–152, 156
short and distort, 133
short interest, 131
short options, 175–177
short position, 92–93
speculators, 6
spinning top, 49
spread, 25, 176–177
Sprint, 158
stock selection
  capitalization, 115
  cash flow, 114

core earnings, 107
debt ratio, 116
diversification, 108–109, 176, 189,
    190–192
dividend yield, 111, 114
indicators, 110–119
price volatility, 119–123
rules of thumb, 105–110
Stockcharts.com, 63
stop orders, 90
straddle, 176–177
strike price of options, 138
supply and demand, 26–27
support and resistance,
    25–29, 33

T

T. Rowe Price, 99
TD Ameritrade, 63, 99
TD Waterhouse, 99
technical analysis
  criteria, 117
  defined, 4
  distinguished, 15
  indicators, 110–116
  price volatility, 119
  tests, 105
three black crows, 59–60
three white soldiers, 61–62
time value, 140, 142, 143–146
trading range, 24, 26, 28,
    31–34
trailing stop, 85

U

uncovered call, 173
underlying stock, 138
upper shadow, 48
uptick rule, 128
uptrend, 10–13

V

Vanguard, 99
volatility, 24, 104, 107, 119–123
volume spikes, 75–78

W

Walgreen, 127–128
Wall Street Journal, 98
WallStreet Inc, 99

Wal-Mart, 111, 113, 158
white candlestick, 47

Y

Yahoo, 63, 158

Z

zero-plus tick, 128–129